Voices of
THE WINDRUSH
GENERATION

Voices of
THE WINDRUSH GENERATION

———

The real story told by the
people themselves

DAVID MATTHEWS

535

Published by Blink Publishing
2.25, The Plaza,
535 Kings Road,
Chelsea Harbour,
London, SW10 0SZ

www.blinkpublishing.co.uk

facebook.com/blinkpublishing
twitter.com/blinkpublishing

Hardback – 978-1-788701-34-1
Ebook – 978-1-788701-53-2

A CIP catalogue of this book is available from the British Library.

Designed and set by seagulls.net
Printed and bound by Great Britain by Clays Ltd, Elcograf S.p.A

1 3 5 7 9 10 8 6 4 2

For Barbara Monica Matthews

Contents

FOREWORD

I first came to Britain in 1967 at the tender age of 23 to play for Haslingden Cricket Club in Lancashire, some 19 miles due north of the industrial powerhouse that was Manchester. Known locally for its stone, wool and cotton industries from the 18th century right up to the 1950s, Haslingden was, and still is, by all accounts, a very small town. It seemed to embody everything I associated with the warm beer, balmy summers and village green image of English cricket I'd formed back home in my native Guyana, largely due to Pathé newsreels, hours of listening to cricket on the BBC World Service and, of course, first-hand accounts of fellow West Indians who had already journeyed across the Atlantic like so many Dick Whittingtons.

In those days, British Guiana, as it was then known, was still part of the British Empire. Independence wouldn't come for nearly a decade yet. Arriving in Haslingden I had a sense of not coming to the 'motherland' but drilling down into the mother lode of England, as having already made my Test debut for the West Indies the previous year, and being born and raised in the Caribbean, I had a great sense of being a stranger in a strange land.

But I was not the first West Indian to play for Haslingden. Over three decades earlier, in 1933, Jamaican batsman George Headley had signed as a professional for the club following the West Indies' tour of England, playing for Haslingden until 1939 and ending due to the outbreak of the Second World War.

Defying a colour bar, which had existed since the birth of West Indies cricket in the 1880s, at the beginning of 1948 – six months before the arrival in Britain of the SS *Empire Windrush* – Headley became the first black captain of a West Indies team, albeit for one Test match in Bridgetown, Barbados. And who was the opposition? England.

In his book *The West Indies: Fifty Years of Test Cricket*, Tony Cozier wrote that the prohibition of a black captain was 'historically understandable at a time when it was generally considered by the ruling classes that the black man was not ready for leadership – political, social, sporting or otherwise'. What this colour bar demonstrated, at the dawn of the Windrush generation's evolution, was that West Indians, who would face years of prejudice, discrimination and racism while making a mark in Britain, were exchanging one climate of inequality and hostility for another.

Yet Headley was far from being the only notable West Indian – cricket playing or otherwise – in Britain at the time. Between 1929 and 1938, Trinidadian and West Indies cricket legend Learie Constantine played for Nelson Cricket Club, also in the Lancashire League, and went on to work for the Ministry of Labour and National Service as a Welfare Officer responsible for West Indians employed in

English factories. In 1943, a London hotel manager refused service to Constantine and his family because of their race. Constantine successfully sued the hotel company in a case that would bring about a sea change in UK race relations. In 1954, Constantine – already an accomplished journalist and broadcaster – qualified as a barrister. Two years after I arrived in Britain, Learie became the first black man to sit in the House of Lords.

While playing for Nelson, Constantine invited his friend, countryman and author, C.L.R. James over to help write his autobiography, *Cricket and I*. James, a cricket aficionado, went on to write arguably one of the finest books ever written on the game, *Beyond a Boundary*.

The Grenadian singer and pianist, Leslie 'Hutch' Hutchinson, who lived in Britain for over 40 years, was one of the country's biggest stars during the twenties and thirties. At one point, Hutch was the highest paid entertainer in Britain. At the other end of the spectrum, in 1912, the ground-breaking Jamaican political activist, Marcus Garvey, emigrated to Britain years before the likes of fellow Jamaican and co-founder of cultural theory, Stuart Hall, or Trinidadian Nobel Laureate, V.S. Naipaul, or the Grenadian Dr David Pitt, Britain's first black Parliamentary candidate.

But even before these titans of sports, the arts, academia and politics arrived there was Crimean War heroine, Mary Seacole, a rare female presence in a male-dominated Hall of Fame of pre-Windrush notables. And what of the 'slave soldiers' of the West India Regiment? It is estimated that between 1795 and 1807, 13,400 slaves were bought from West Indian plantations to fight for the regiment in theatres that included the Napoleonic War and the First World War.

What Seacole, legions of West Indian soldiers, and Constantine, James, Hutchinson, Garvey, Hall and Naipaul have in common is that while being born in the Caribbean, they dedicated themselves to British public life. But this is just the tip of a Caribbean iceberg! What about Bill Morris, Baron Morris of Handsworth (Jamaica), the first black leader of a major British trade union? Or Bernie Grant (Guyana), who in 1987 was one of three of Britain's first black MPs? Or former Attorney-General, Patricia Scotland QC (Dominica), or Baroness Valerie Amos (Guyana) who, as Director of SOAS, is the first black woman to head a UK university?

From decade to decade, century to century, West Indians have educated, entertained, inspired and led in Britain, regardless of colour or creed, without fear or favour. Because of my cricketing career – both on and off the field – since the early 1960s and, I guess, reaching its apex in the glory days of West Indies cricket from the 1970s to the 1990s, I have very much been associated with being Guyanese, West Indian and African-Caribbean. During that period of global cricketing success, I captained the West Indies from 1974 to 1985 and was constantly reminded of the role, and the responsibility, that the Windies had in instilling a sense of pride in Britain's Caribbean community, a community that at times felt dislocated from its roots and under threat from a hostile environment.

But triumphs on the field or ennoblement or elevation through the ranks is just one small part of the Windrush story. The silent majority who migrated to Britain from the Caribbean from 1948 onwards are unsung heroes, only known, in the main, to their families, friends, colleagues and local communities. They are not celebrities or in the public eye. They are ordinary people who have made an extraordinary contribution to Britain. To that end, the stories in this book are a vital recognition of their tremendous efforts and sacrifices. To count myself among their number is an honour.

Sir Clive Lloyd, CBE, *September 2018*

INTRODUCTION

'David, have you met Big John? Big John was on the Windrush, you know. Oh yes. He's been doing the rounds this year. The media can't get enough of him.'

Big John is, indeed, BIG. Even at 92, and with the moderate help of a walking stick that looks like it has been carved from an old oak tree with his bare hands, he stands a good six feet four in anyone's currency. In an era of celebrity hyperbole, 'living legend' has become something of a cliché. But Big John is just that: a Jamaican Odysseus, an adventurer who had set sail in '48 with a few hundred of his countrymen and crossed the Atlantic in search of his very own Ithaca, thus helping to change the course of British history.

'Big John, it's an absolute pleasure.' I hesitated to say much else as he took a slow, plaintive sip from a tumbler of Appleton's finest. We were sitting in the Learie Constantine Centre (LCC) in Willesden, a social club for the local West Indian cognoscenti. 'Good to meet you, David.' Big John leant back in his chair, taking over its delicate frame like a one-man army of occupation. Big John.

'Have you seen that photo of that dapper young man on the *Windrush* in a pinstripe suit?' said Norman, the club's chairman, as he ordered another round of drinks for our small intergenerational group. 'It's famous. *That's* Big John.'

Having got Big John's age, I couldn't resist a tease. 'I just interviewed another Norman, Norman Mitchell. Do you know him? Lives up the road in Harlesden. He's 98. You're a mere spring chicken.' Big John chuckled the chuckle of a man who had been there, done that, bought the T-shirt, made the T-shirt, sold the T-shirt... He was gruff, warm, gravelly, ancient. They certainly didn't make 'em like Big John any more.

I became an irregular at the LCC having fallen into the wake of the so-called 'Windrush scandal', which, in the early part of 2018, had exposed the Conservative government's immigration policy, known to many as the 'hostile environment', which had resulted in the intimidation, isolation and ultimately deportation of hundreds, possibly thousands, who knew? No records had been kept, apparently. People who had come in the fifties, sixties and seventies and had spent decades in Britain, worked here, bought property here, married and raised families here were being tossed aside like old boots.

My parents were of that generation. They came from what was then called British Guiana, in 1962. The clue is in the name. My mother's passport was issued at the Police Headquarters in Georgetown, the capital, on 3 January 1962. Three days later she was on a plane to the UK.

I was born in Hackney, in London's East End, in 1967. The first time I visited what was now, thanks to independence, called 'Guyana', was the Christmas of 1974. I spent six weeks there with my parents, staying with cousins who, it felt like, teased, tormented and tortured me for most of my stay. I got bitten by some unseen bug and developed a puss-filled dome on my right ankle the size of the O2 Arena. I had a fever for days. During the trip, two of my father's cousins drowned in a fishing accident out in the Atlantic. I met my maternal grandmother, the daughter of Portuguese immigrants. She had long black hair. I think the realisation that she was white traumatised me. I didn't return to Guyana until January 2018.

Shortly after my return, I discovered that my mother had died, just short of her 77th birthday, alone in her little flat, while I was away. We hadn't had the closest of relationships over the years. My father had died, in Guyana, in 2003. It was nine months before I had learned of his death. Aged 50, I was now an orphan.

And then the Windrush scandal broke.

I say it 'broke', but I had reported on the horrors of the UK's Caribbean deportations some 25 years earlier as a reporter for the *Caribbean Times* – a weekly newspaper that was essential reading for Britain's ex-pat West Indian community. I remember one story I covered, which had been championed by the late MP for Tottenham, himself a Guyanese ex-pat, Bernie Grant. Between Bernie, *Caribbean Times* and God knows how many unheralded individuals of the day, a young girl who was born in Jamaica had won indefinite leave to remain. To cut a long immigration story short (they are never succinct), the girl's mother and father had separated, but her mother had returned to Jamaica. Her father had leave to remain, but she didn't. The Home Office, in its wisdom, had decided that the young girl should go back to Jamaica to be reunited with her mother, despite the fact that her mother did not want her and she had spent most of her life growing up in London.

We convened on the steps of Tottenham Town Hall for a triumphant photo op. There were maybe half a dozen of us. There was no fanfare. This was business as usual.

Cut to a quarter of a century later, and Tottenham MP David Lammy, whose parents also hailed from Guyana (we are a truculent bunch), has been leading a campaign for justice for the legion of people *sans papiers* – denied status, healthcare, pensions, sacked from work, jailed, separated from kith and kin, deported, humiliated. While in Britain we mock US President Donald Trump and his muscular immigration policies of threatened border walls and actual incarceration of children, shorn from their parents, in Britain, quietly, determinedly, passive aggressively, we do the same, and worse, in the name of the Crown.

But this is no party political affair. As righteous as David Lammy's campaign is, Labour is not without sin. As home secretary from June 2009 to May 2010, Labour's Alan Johnson oversaw the expulsion of an unknown number of the Windrush generation, many of whom are now sadly dead and gone. Dubbed, 'a deeply principled working-class hero' by the *Daily Mail*, you'd think Johnson would know better. But when it comes to party politics, there ain't no black in blue or red.

By the early spring of 2018, the more inquisitive corners of the British news media had got the bit between its teeth. The *Guardian* to the BBC began sniffing around. People started to come forward, now emboldened by the fact that the immigration genie was out of the bottle. But much as how the *Daily Mail* had once ridden into town claiming victory for bringing, in part, the murderers of Stephen Lawrence to book, once again the British news media was taking credit for spearheading a campaign that many under-resourced, over-stretched hacks, activists, families and individuals had fought for decades with little mainstream public attention. *Plus ça change.* That's not to say that the big beasts of British journalism don't deserve a pat on the back for going hard at the government. The *Guardian*'s Gary Younge (of Bajan descent) and Channel 4 News correspondent Simon Israel (non-Caribbean) had produced some sterling reportage, which, along with David Lammy and others, has resulted in the scalp of at least one bumbling Home Secretary, Amber Rudd, and national and international shame being heaped on an establishment that loves to peddle the myth of Britain being a 'tolerant' country.

But enough of all that.

This book isn't about scandal; it's about honour, respect, homage. It is, in its own small way, about settling a personal score as much as a professional duty.

In the last couple of years of my mother's life, I regularly tapped her up for information about our family history. Often, her memory was fuzzy, partly thanks to the passage of time, partly because of selective amnesia. But if there was any legacy I could fulfil for my children, beyond a series of scribblings unlikely to ever see royalties in their lifetime, let alone mine, it is the legacy of a cultural identity inherited from my parents. Identity. It gets such a bad press these days. Identity is seen as a sort of pick-and-mix thing. It's non-binary, non-binding, amorphous. Anyone can be anything they choose to be. Just so long as they are not *sans papiers.*

For people of my generation – and my children's generations, Windrush 2.0 and 3.0, if you will – a far more pragmatic identity is not just desirable, it's essential for the community's survival. Going through my mother's effects was an exercise in not Black History Month, but black history. Period. Old photographs, airmail letters, birth certificates, passports – all the usual stuff – but also, what seems at first sight, *ephemeralia*, a romantic attachment to bank statements from the 1960s, mortgage payment slips from the 1970s, utility bills, diaries, scribbled notes and contacts books, wage slips and employment correspondence, and home improvement invoices and what have you spanning decades, all crammed into brown envelope after plastic bag after crumbling manila folder. Why had she kept this stuff? Yes, in later years, she had become something of a hoarder. But thinking back to my childhood, she, and my father to a lesser extent, had always maintained a burgeoning personal bureaucracy, as well as a kaleidoscopic array of knick-knacks and curios, ranging from tools designed for jobs that no longer existed to the de rigueur drinks cabinet and a stuffed sloth, somehow brought all the way over from Guyana in the seventies without question. One must remember, however, that these were the days when you could smoke on an aeroplane. Indeed, in those days, you could pretty much do anuything on an aeroplane.

What I have come to realise is, what could easily be dismissed as junk, or tat, or a waste of money, all amounted to *evidence* – not so much of a life lived, as status achieved. And by status, I don't mean class, I mean one's position relative to the general scheme of things; or put another way, 'identity'. For all the pre-internet shonkiness of keeping all those bags of paperwork, in light of recent events, the Windrush generation was, for the most part, hip to keeping records and proof of their status. They knew the writing was on the wall. Coming from an arbitrary world of smash-and-grab colonialism, the Windrush generation knew the importance of having an identity, figuratively and literally.

In recent years we have seen the fallout of lost identity. In my own, occasionally clumsy way, I have tried to investigate, interrogate, prod, poke and provoke discussion around the hot topic of the British West Indian or African-Caribbean community's identity, in print, on TV and radio, not because it makes good copy or frightfully jolly conversation, but because I have a personal stake in it. When I look around, the community I see is not the one I grew up in. The hostile environment notwithstanding, it is dwindling, in decline and being assailed by African-American cultural imperialism and 'black culture' – whatever the hell that is.

I freely admit that I feel ashamed of my own role in all of this. It's not so much what I've done that I feel guilty about; it's what I haven't done. As the philosopher John Stuart Mill said, 'Bad men need nothing more to compass their ends, than that good men should look on and do nothing.' By talking to the contributors you are about to hear from in this book, in a concerted and deliberate way, I have come to appreciate that the challenges my parents endured, not just coming here, but under the colonial system they escaped, hardened them in ways that inevitably had a knock-on effect on my wellbeing but which, with hindsight, and a better education, access to resources and a greater understanding of the world than they had, I should have helped them to navigate their way through Britain better, rather than spend so much of my time rebelling. Maybe I am alone in feeling this way. Maybe not. But I can't help but think that by resenting the quiet humiliations my parents faced, both in Britain and 'back a yard', a number of my generation has helped to incubate and empower elements of Windrush 3.0 and now 4.0 with a 'f*** you' mentality borne of a lack of identity, an absence of self-awareness and a crushed sense of insight and empathy.

With that mea culpa in mind, one aim of this book is to let go of that pain and give a voice to a generation that for all too long has been voiceless beyond the walled gardens of Britain's West Indian communities in Hackney, Brixton, Handsworth, Toxteth, Chapeltown and the like. Rather than second-guess or 'report' on what people within the community have to say, why not let them just speak for themselves, about what the hell they want to talk about?

To this end, this is the beauty of oral history.

During much of the Windrush generation's evolution, oral history has, according to *The Oxford Handbook of Oral History*, 'moved from the periphery to the mainstream of academic studies, being employed as a research tool by historians, anthropologists, sociologists, medical therapists, documentary film makers, and educators at all levels'. For the wider Windrush community – from the first generation right up to the present-day fourth generation – whici often feels like it's on the fringes of mainstream British society, and thus lacks a voice or a fair crack in the media, politics and public life, oral history has become a powerful means of narrating the experiences of those whose value cannot be measured by clicks, likes or hits.

In some ways, this book is an African-Caribbean homage to Studs Terkel's *Working: People Talk About What They Do All Day and How They Feel About What They Do,* save for the fact that the stories aren't just about the contributors' working lives. The similarity with Terkel's approach to oral history is that this collection of personal stories is very much that – personal. West Indians have an idiosyncratic way of telling stories, shifting from one subject to another – back and forth, back and forth – going off on tangents before resolving themselves with a moral flourish, like an *Aesop's Fable.* Jean-Luc Godard's maxim – 'a story should have a beginning, a middle and an end, but not necessarily in that order' – must've been contrived while on holiday in the Caribbean. Part of this non-linear approach to communication invariably comes from centuries of oral tradition, word play, vocal dexterity, and the narrative teasing and taunting, beloved of West Indian raconteurs, which is known as 'picong' – a form of banter that's a bit like the dozens, only not done in duologue or nearly as offensive to one's mother.

But oral history is not without its flaws, or at least, leaps of faith.

As an interviewer, the moment I interpret or interrogate what my sparring partner has to say for him or herself with more than natural curiosity, or scepticism, the moment doubt or cynicism takes me away from listening and bullies me into questioning, is the moment the oral history contract is broken and a new one is formed based on hard and fast principles of journalism. Oral history does not produce the sort of scripted, fact-checked, critical exposition, as exemplified by some hack named David Matthews writing about the cultural conservatism of the Windrush generation in the *New Statesman* in November 2007:

In many respects, Afro-Caribbean and African people are tailor-made for the Tory Party. It was the Tories who introduced the 1948 British Nationality Act, which gave all members of the Commonwealth the right to British citizenship and kick-started mass immigration into the UK. In the summer of that year, 492 Jamaicans stepped off the *Empire Windrush* at Tilbury Docks and a new ethnic community in Britain was born. Britain was a cold, austere and hostile place for foreigners, but it was a Tory Shadow Home Secretary, David Maxwell Fyfe, who welcomed the arrivals with warm words: 'We are proud that we impose no colour-bar restrictions. We must maintain our great metropolitan traditions of hospitality to everyone from every part of the empire.'

Despite an open-door policy, Caribbean immigration was at first a trickle, with annual figures in the low hundreds. The adoptive country of choice for most West Indians was the US. But following the McCarran-Walter Act in 1952, which restricted entry into America, UK immigration increased steadily.

The stories you are about to read come from the hearts, minds and lips of people simply telling it as it is: how they see it, how they saw it, how they experienced it. Remarkably, but for some foggy recollections about exact dates or ships' names, due diligence suggests a higher than average appreciation for the facts among the people I met. Some recollections are so vivid that they put you right there, in the moment, in a cane field one minute, a grubby factory floor the next.

Linguistically, I've tried to stay true to the dulcet tones and nuances of the West Indian brogue. However, the written word can never do justice to Caribbean dialect, which can range from a darker shade of a Bristolian or Cornish accent (Barbados) up through the Windward Islands to the mystical Kwéyòl (Dominica) and westward to Jamaica and a patois that pervades global popular culture. But given the fine line between an authentic reproduction of 'back-a-yard' speech and clunky Caribbean caricature, I've been mindful to give the book's storytellers a generous touch of linguistic Encona rather than drown the reader in red-hot pidgin English. Accents aside, West Indians of my parents' generation speak with impeccable diction. As an East Ender, I was forever pulled up by my folks for dropping my aitches and turning every 'TH' into an 'F'. If anything, to hear a Windrusher turn on a heavy yard accent is as much an affectation as Jamie 'jerk rice' Oliver's mockney marketing shtick.

As the crow flies, the distance from Jamaica to Guyana – one end of what was once known as the British West Indies to another – is some 1,500 miles, or equivalent to London to Vienna. The current population of the West Indies is around six million, with the West Indian community in Britain numbering just over a million. As politically incorrect as 'West Indian' may seem, it's important to differentiate it, at least for this book, from the term 'Caribbean', which as a region is home to some 45 million people. In other words, the West Indies and the Caribbean are two very different things. I don't know anyone from Haiti or Cuba, despite those two islands accounting for half the population of the Caribbean. In countless years of travelling to Barbados for winter holidays, I've never run into anyone from Puerto Rico. And I can count on NO hands the last time I ate in a Guadeloupean, Martinican or United States Virgin Islands restaurant. The point is, based on Powellian arguments against 'whip-handed' West Indian immigration, decades of organised racist policy and practice and the ill-treatment of the Windrush generation up to today, it's worth putting that community into some sort of perspective, especially when measured against the hundreds of millions of people from the European Union who have had an automatic right of entry to the UK, since the Maastricht Treaty came into force in 1993.

The point should also be made that the stories in this book are *not* the definitive story of West Indians, African-Caribbeans or people from the Caribbean in Britain, or the history of people of African descent in the British Isles. There are other far loftier tomes that deal with African Roman legionnaires or the decline and fall and renaissance of pre-Windrush black communities in Cardiff, Liverpool or Bristol. I know from personal experience that West Indians were coming and going from these shores long before the SS *Empire Windrush* set sail in '48. My grandfather, Sir Kenneth Sievewright Stoby, who went on to become the Chief Justice of Guyana and then Barbados, for instance, first came to Britain in 1926, with his father, William, who by all accounts was of Scottish ancestry anyway. My great-uncle, Percy Sievewright Stoby, was a decorated sergeant who served in the London Regiment in the First World War and was Mayor of Beddington and Wallington from 1951 to 1952. Another great-uncle, Ivan, was a 2nd lieutenant in the Second World War. In 1920, aged 12, another great-uncle, Eric Sievewright Stoby, was shipped off to Truro College in Cornwall...

You get the picture.

Like most West Indians, the Matthews-Stoby-Dey-Skeete-Towler-von Schultz family axis is a tale of admixture, exploration, exploitation, adventure and upheaval; but the origins of such tales lie in a history of transatlantic comings and goings dating back centuries. To paraphrase Malcolm X: we didn't land on Plymouth Sound, Plymouth Sound landed on us. In an age in which those of us known as 'the other' are still routinely questioned in Britain about our status, rights, contributions, commitment and even our capacity to understand the English sense of humour, it is perhaps 'ironic' that the Windrush generation has merely headed back in the direction whence its unwitting Pilgrim Forefathers came centuries earlier. The way that I see it, the Windrush generation are not immigrants. Nor are they economic migrants. They are more than that. They are pioneers who forged a path out of the moral, political and economic bankruptcy of a rapacious colonial era. Many were born into poverty – and were destined to remain in it – until they came to Britain in search of a better life. In return, they gave their blood, sweat and tears. Seventy years on from when the SS *Empire Windrush* set sail from Jamaica, their journey hasn't ended. Successive generations of sons and daughters, doctors and nurses, train drivers, cab drivers, carpenters, builders, lawyers, footballers, cricketers, singers, actors and, dare I say, writers, demonstrate that the journey has only just begun.

NICEY AND JENNY

Nicey and her daughter Jenny were both born in Jamaica. But as was common for West Indian immigrant families in the 1950s and '60s, Jenny and her siblings were separated from her mum and dad for several months, and even years, as her parents laid a foundation in Britain for the family.

Life was easy growing up in Jamaica. When you're a child you don't really know the difference!

We had far to walk to school in the mornings – we had to walk more than a mile. But first we would have to get water from the well, which was three quarters of a mile from where we lived.

I was born in 1936. My first memories are of living with my grandmother. I then left her and went to live with my dad in the capital, Kingston. Then, about ten years old, I came back to look after my granny. In the mornings I had to get up, make her breakfast, get the bucket, go to the well and come back, get my hair plaited … and then I was off to school. When school was finished, I had no time to dilly-dally. I had to get home, collect wood, and then come back and get dinner ready.

Mum, you had to cook dinner aged ten years old?

Yes, I think my granny was a bit … it was a lazy thing, you know?!

Perhaps in those times it was more a matter of, 'You're a child, do as I say?'

It was strict. She would go to bed when the sun was still shining outside, and she would still expect me to go to bed as well. Hahaha!

I grew up far away from the town, in Santa Cruz, St Elizabeth, which is towards the end of Jamaica, down, deep inland. There were a lot of different people living in the area, but it was mostly family where we were. The brother of my grandfather and his children lived nearby.

So, we lived here, my cousin lived just down there, and over the same side lived my great-grand-uncle, and his children lived further down there… It was like a circle of family.

I don't have a clue when my granny was born. They don't talk about your age. Not even me; she wouldn't talk about how old I was. She used to joke, 'You going to turn woman, child?'

Grandad was probably born in the early 1900s, which would have made him approximately 36 years old when he had you.

He died in 1961/62 when he was about 57 years old.

And you were the youngest child weren't you, Mum?

Yes. On my dad's side, he had three of us: me, Maurice and older sister, Vera. But on my mum's side, there was Sidney, Pearly, Lynette, Clunis, Carrol and Basil.

It's difficult to replicate the way the indigenous population lives in the UK, and how it views the possibility, even nowadays, of a woman having children with different men. It's looked down on, it's a difficult dynamic.

We didn't grow up together. Me and Vera spent a little time together with my dad's mother before I went to Kingston. And then I went to Kingston and left Vera with my granny. She was there for a long time. And when I came back to the country, she then went to Kingston. So, then me and Maurice got together, and again she came up. He went to a different school to me. I got to adulthood before I got to know some of my other siblings. I knew my mother had them, but we were in different places.

In Jamaica, you don't know some of your siblings until you get big, and then you hear from someone, 'That's your sister' or 'that's your brother'. Up to now, there's still one of them I don't know. When my mum passed, and I went to her funeral, he didn't come, so I still don't know him.

When I was still small, and going to school, my biggest sister had started having children. Whether she was married or not, I don't know. Or she could have married after?

Mum, Granny – we call her 'Gunga' – and your dad weren't married, were they?

No. She didn't marry the father of the first two children either. I don't know if my mum was in the church during her younger years. I don't know if she was into the church, when she was having children.

What, Gunga? In her younger years? Was she a bit wild?

I don't think so, because when she was ready, she would up and go on her 'pilgrimage'.

Mum said Granny would always be on her pilgrimage. But that pilgrimage suggests religion, doesn't it?

Yes, but when she finished with all her … hahahahaha!

So, when she had finished all of her 'goodness', she would go and repent somewhere?

I think she liked having the kids, but I don't think she was the type of person who liked looking after them.

It wasn't a bad childhood. We had clothes and plenty of food. And my dad used to send money home to support.

But it was also a difficult childhood. Because we've spoken about how difficult it was for children back in those times. Parents were always in total control, weren't they, Mum?

Yeah. You don't have any say. You couldn't ask Granny her age – she wouldn't talk about anything like that. And you couldn't answer back. If anybody came and say that you did something wrong, and you know that you didn't do it, you couldn't tell them that you didn't do it. Because the first thing they would do is give you a lashing. It was strict, and there were licks.

I remember coming from school with one of my cousins. We were playing and she hit me. I felt it and I said, 'Stop, I'm finished. I'm not playing!' But she continued to hit me. So, I ran her down and give her a good beating and her granny took her around to my granny. And me and that girl are still family. My granny back me up in the room that night, and they don't care where they hit you.

She waited until I came in … and gave me some licks. And I said, *'All right, wait until tomorrow. When I go to school and catch my cousin,*

I'm going to give her one beating.' I couldn't tell my granny that. I told her to stop.

I think the hard attitude came from the older people, from slavery days and what have you, because those times the men didn't think children were supposed to go to school. They was supposed to go to the bush to work. They didn't like sending children to school in those days. They'd say, 'You can't go to school today – you have to help me plant corn.' You'd have to go. What were you supposed to do? You can't say no. There weren't any rules and nobody to defend the children.

Even in the UK, rules about children didn't come in until recently, and so I think in the West Indies we had a lot of the Victorian attitudes to children. I hear this, not just from my mum, but from other older people. Anybody could catch you and beat you if they thought you had done something wrong. It was like a free-for-all at that time.

Every evening I had to put my father's mug of coffee on the table, in time for when he returned home from work. That evening, me and my brother Maurice were talking, but I didn't realise the time had gone so far. Then I looked and saw that my dad was coming, I started to tremble. There was the motor tyre over the door. And I knew he was going to beat me. I was edging to the door, to get out, whilst he was stretching up for the motor tyre. But he managed to slip up. He ran me down and caught up with me, then I got away, and then he fell down. I went and walked about. When I returned home that same night, he had gone to meet his lady friend – he hadn't married yet. And when I came back, Maurice was sitting there alone, so we talked until we heard them coming up the road to the house. I slipped back behind the house. There was nowhere else to go. And this lady came with them and asked for me. She said I should come. He told her what happened. And the lady said, 'Oh, Mr Mullins, don't bother beat her again, for it gone.' And he said, 'Me! Me! Me! The only way I don't beat her is if I don't catch her tonight!'

Hearing everything made my heart sink. So, they were there talking, talking until the lady left. They had a fowl coop, with the mesh, which was high up on stilts. So I went behind it, and both came out looking for me. My father went in the kitchen, and she saw my foot there, and she picked up a pebble and threw it on my foot to indicate to my dad where I was. And I tell you, what that man did was really cruel. They caught me, he held me, and he was a six-footer man, and he gave me some beatings with the motor tyre inner tube, and when you look at my skin… When he finished beating me, he gave me a bucket, and this was about ten o'clock at night, to go and get water. And the water's not just down the road there – you have to go down into a gully and then climb up to the pipe to get the water. I could have fallen down.

When I grew up and thought about it, I thought that was very, very cruel. At that time, I could have been 12 years old or so. If I was even that old. And I had to go and get the water and carry it back. And the next day you could see all my skin bruised.

That must have been quite sad for you Mum, and embarrassing as well, because you've got to go to school.

And it's not like here. Nobody cares. The teacher didn't ask what happened to me. Nobody did. And when I got big, I thought about it, and it was very cruel. It's not just that he beat me, he sent me for water where anybody could have attacked me.

My grandparents' parents were probably emerging from slavery. When things are done to you, the only thing you have to call upon is your own experience. So, if your own experiences are let's just spank this out of you, you don't have any idea that you can negotiate. There's no idea of that, so you can only act the way you experience. That's what I believe, anyway.

I didn't have anybody to say, 'That's enough' or 'No, you can't send her for water at this time of the night.' Nobody there to say something.

Because you lived with your dad and he was master, and even if there was a woman there, the likelihood is that she will do what he wanted to do because it was very male-dominated.

I can't understand how after so long in the evening he didn't cool down.

It's anger, isn't it?

I remember times when I ask Jenny and the others to do something before they go to school. They'd gone off to school without doing the thing I asked them to do. And, whilst they're at school, I'm in the house quarrelling, 'Wait till they come back!' but by the time they get back from school, I've already cooled down. I don't even mention it. So, I don't understand how he didn't calm down.

I feel it's psychological and anger; frustration hurts all inside, but you don't even know you're carrying that. He might not even have realised. I think it's more deep-seated in that generation. In a way, my dad was quite an angry person, too. He passed away last year, just before his 95th birthday. He was 15 years older than you wasn't he, Mum? He was quite an angry person. It's only when he got much older that he became calmer, but the anger was still simmering. I feel that people of my dad's era, and going back slightly further, they had these feelings but didn't know what to do with them. He wasn't sure what was happening, and his experience was even tougher than maybe my mum's. My dad would have been 15 years old at the time my mum was born. Dad was born in 1922. If it was a free-for-all at my mum's age, imagine what it was like for my dad. Growing up must have been difficult for my dad.

Dad's father, Masstram, once sent one of his sons to Santa Cruz to get something before school, but he didn't come back quickly enough. So, Masstram borrowed the teacher's strap and beat the boy in front of the school. Could you imagine that embarrassment? They're not thinking about that.

He wasn't even a boy, he was around 16 years old? Maybe it's because of anger at what happened to him?

They don't show their love, but they care for you, in their own way.

Maybe it's a weakness or something for that generation. When I think about my dad, the tactile type of love came from Mum. He was a hard worker, and he provided. He did the sort of things back in those days men of his age group wouldn't do, like, for example, he would help Mum to wash the clothes. But, in terms of hugging, we wouldn't get that from him. It was only when we left home and we were grown, and we were always going back that we started to hug him, but he kind of started to do it then so it took him years because there was just a lot of stuff that had happened in his youth. He kept it inside and didn't put it anywhere and it just made him a very stern person. We felt we knew that Dad loved us but he didn't show it at all. In terms of hugging, it always came from Mum. It took my dad years to show love.

And you couldn't tell him that there was an open evening because he was so tired he wouldn't want to go.

Different mentality. We didn't play sports together or go fishing ... he didn't do any of that. He provided. That was it. He went to work and brought the money home but in terms of interaction with us there would be conversations and talking but there wasn't any participation. We would all sit and watch cricket or boxing on the TV. One of my first abiding memories of being over here was sitting on my dad's lap watching the Muhammad Ali fight on TV. I spoke about it in his eulogy. I remember my dad shadow boxing, copying Ali's moves, and when Muhammad Ali landed a knockout punch he jumped up, and in the excitement I fell on the floor!

I never went further than sixth form. I used to go to school for four days a week and come back to the country because my granny said that I wasn't learning anything at school on a Friday. So, she made me stay home and wash my school clothes.

It's funny, if you weren't learning anything, it was safe to stay home, like education wasn't that important for girls. Do you think that was the case for women then?

Must be the case... When I finished school, my dad said to send me to learn to sew, but Granny wouldn't hear of it.

That was Grandma ... again, Victorian attitudes.

She wouldn't hear of it. She got the idea I wouldn't come back in time, and I am going to have a man! At the time, I was a child and they weren't corresponding with me. I had an uncle who used to send money and nothing come of it.

I always said that if my mum was born in a different era she's clever enough to have had a profession if she had been of a different era but saying that there have been other women that have been successful where education was valued and a woman getting a profession was valued but in my grandparents' eyes it seems that Mum getting any further education was not that important. What did Grandpa do?

He used to work in a hospital as a porter, and I don't know what my grandma did. We didn't have any books around.

School was very strict. If you're a bit late, the teacher would stand on the veranda with the strap and you had to hold your hand out and you'd get beaten. Sometimes I used to have a bottle of water, so I'd put the water on myself to make it look like I was sweating and breathing hard, and they give you a break. I always had to be rushing 'cause there was so many things to do in the morning before school. I had to do work and there was no bus to take me to school – I had to walk. There were children that came further than me to get to school. When you think about it, life wasn't easy.

They took every little thing from Jamaica and bring it here. They [the British] never used to do anything. The road was so bad, they used to pay people to break stones, and it was those stones for the main road. The district road was made of broken stones. They paid people little or nothing for that. They didn't do anything good out there, really.

We used to have a radio, and I used to hear about how much money was going to England. When you think about it, we don't have any money, yet you hear about how much leaving from there? It wasn't easy.

They used to treat the farmers bad. And the people with the bananas had to plant from when it's small. Not outside the parish though.

So, each parish would grow different vegetables?

They used to pay the farmers next to nothing for a whole long bunch, with six 'hand' of banana.

Seems like they took a lot and gave very little in return. Did you have contact with many white people before you came here?

Oh yes. There was one who lived near Santa Cruz, named Demshon. He had his own plane. They lived high up, in the better parts. Sometimes he used to come to Santa Cruz in his sharp pants with his big cigar. He used to have a racecourse with horses. There were English people in Kingston, but I didn't have family who worked with any of them. But, you knew where they were living. They lived in the best part, nice big houses.

I was 16 years old when I left school.

Sixteen seems to be quite an old age to be leaving school in the West Indies. Because even in the UK, children were finishing school at 14 years old.

First class, second class, third class, fourth class, that's what they call it out there.

Did you do any exams?

No!

Maybe sixth form represent something different, not a sixth form as we know it here.

Out there they call it first class, second class, third class, fourth class. So, when you reach sixth class...

So, back in the days, it was more like when you finished you were in sixth class?

Yes.

So, the years would be like class would be the equivalent to our school years. I would imagine that's before you go to secondary school?

I wanted to get a nice job, travel, to make a decent life. It entered my mind to come to Britain, before your daddy said he wanted us to come here.

Before you met Dad?

Before he got the chance. I was 28 years old when I came.

Because you came in 1964. Yes, because my second youngest sister, Beverley was born in January 1964. And you came in June 1964. Dad had come a year before you, when you were pregnant. Dad must have left in June 1963, because I think that's what his passport says. Beverley was very young when you left – three or four months old. Something like that?

Yeah. Before I met my husband, I was working at a hairdressers' down in Santa Cruz…

I didn't know that!

And when I met Dad, I was still working for a teacher, as a cook in his house.

A bit like a housekeeper?

You do what is available, to make the money. Finding work wasn't easy. We made bulla cake, to sell. Even the teacher at school used to make bulla cake.

I did leave Granny before I met your dad. I don't know if she was getting off her head or what! She was sending me to her brother to work for him. One day, I was using a big wooden bowl, and she just came and dragged the bowl away from me. Remember, I am a child. So, maybe that time she was going off her head, I don't know. I looked at her and said, 'You're a wicked and cruel old lady.' I did say that.

Maybe there were other things in there as well, Mum! Maybe this is the sensitised version!

No, I didn't say anything bad. For those times, I couldn't say anything like that.

And then, I went off. And when I came back, my aunt told me that she don't know where I can go tonight because my granny was going to beat me. So, I decided that she was not going to beat me, and my eye can't see anywhere, and I'm not going in there. My cousins were just down the road and I stayed there for a couple of days, and then I went to my mother's sister for a time, and then I found my mother and then I joined back up with her.

Mother was about. She was absent for a long time. One of my father's sisters had adopted me from her. I don't know how old I was then. I remember she woke me up and put me outside, because I had wet the bed. She opened the door and put me outside in the middle of the night and locked the door.

Your dad's sister adopted you, from Gunga? That was something that happened quite a lot [in the Caribbean].

They said she had a daughter, and the child died. I must have reminded her of that child. I can't even say how old I was. But, I can remember that she came and woke me up. I wet the bed, she opened the door and the moon was shining. I stood at the side of the house, and I looked out and there were lots of white rabbits. They were feeding on the lawn. And I was outside a long time. And then she opened the door and let me back in. I don't know how old I was.

Was that before you went to live in Kingston with your dad? Maybe she adopted you at quite a young age?

Then she left me with my granny. Then my father sent for me to come to Kingston.

I never grew up with my mum anytime, until I was big.

It wasn't just you was it, Mum? It was the other siblings as well wasn't it?

Like I said Jen, she loved having kids, but she didn't like looking after them. I didn't have relationships with my brother and sisters.

I suppose even the relationship with your mum must have been hit and miss.

The relationship wasn't that good.

I get a sense that for you, growing up, there was no stability.

He sent me back home because his sister, who was there looking after the mother, came to Kingston; she didn't have anybody there and so he sent me back to the country. There was a lot of moving up and down, from one person to the next.

And now when I think about the impact the instability later has on them, it's quite high, isn't it?

Yeah, but I can still thank God, I had my head screwed on.

You had lots of resilience.

That's why when I came here, the most important thing was to get them [her siblings]. They were with my mum, and knowing my mum I didn't want her to pass them on to somebody.

I met Basil [her husband] at a fairground. He saw me and asked someone who I was.

See, my mum was a bit of a stunner!

And then he found out who I was, and then he started to visit. They had a fair, you would dance, they had the maypole and the fairground. I knew people there. I was living with my mum at age 21 or 22 when I met Bas.

At that age, Mum had Carlton in 1956.

That wasn't a relationship [with Carlton's father]. Elders didn't tell you anything about men and relationships. The father went off on a pilgrimage, and came back with another pregnant lady.

Jamaica has the most churches of any country, like one every half a mile or something like that.

The men who were supposed to be the pastors were supposed to be teaching, instead of taking advantage of the young ladies.

I think maybe religion is a form of control isn't it?

When we married, how old was I again? It was in 1960.

So you married in March 1960, and I was born in June 1960. And Balford, my older brother who passed away, was born in 1957. For Mum and Dad there are six of us: four girls and two boys. And Carlton was away from my dad, and he had two older sons away from my mum.

Bas was a farmer. My dad and his other brothers went to the South in America twice to work in fruit picking. He came back and some of that money was used to buy the Rochester land, Rochester being the family name. I'm Isaac-George now, but Rochester is the family name. So, they had land. My dad's father was a tailor, and my dad's mum was a housekeeper in Kingston. My dad's elder brother must have come over here just after the Windrush in 1948? He took ages before he sent for my dad. He sent for him in 1963. It took a long time. He sent for other people first.

When things are established within the family, and seeps itself into the psyche in a way, you think you have control, but it's something that is passed down from generation to generation.

You hoped that your life would be better in Britain.

Did you think of Queen and country when you came here, Mum?

No! We came here to work and help yourself.

My dad came with the idea to work; he wasn't recruited. Daddy didn't want us to come because he said he wasn't staying.

But I said they had to come. Bas wasn't recruited. He was sent for by his brother.

Daddy was sent for by his brother, who was here by himself for a long time. He sent for his wife, and by then he had children. And he sent for his wife's brother. My dad's father still lived in Jamaica and was ill. And my dad was sent for in 1963.

Dad started to look for his papers in 1962. When Dad came, I was home in Jamaica with the children. He just wanted to send for me. And I came, but I said we had to send for the kids. But we had big arguments because he said 'we were going home, we're not staying'. Then I said, we can't, there's no money, there's nothing to go home to. We worked and saved to send for Jenny and Balford first. I think he wanted to come and work for money and then go back home. I left the children with my mum and I didn't want my mum to give them to somebody.

It was hard to leave the children. And that's why, when I got the chance, I decided to send for them. I left the baby with my mum, at age four to five months old.

Beverley was born in 1964, because she was about six months when you came. And straight away, then you became pregnant and Selina was born in May 1965.

It was very, very hard. Some of the Windrush generation came with their children. I think after I sent for Beverley and Gloria, the immigration rules changed, which is why it was harder to get Carlton. He finally came when he was a grown man.

When I first came, I worked in a tea flask factory near Spurs. I got that job after I had the baby [Selina]. I was getting about £3–4 per week.

I arrived by plane, and it was the first time I'd ever been on a plane. When I got on the plane, I was thinking about when I'd see my children again. I was just thinking about what was happening to them. I was thinking, 'What have I done?' when you come and see the situation. One little room, one chair, one table. Then you're unexpectedly sharing the kitchen with a whole lot of other people. I wasn't used to it. They keep opening the door and leave it. Back home you don't lock the door. Only at night you close your door.

It was Ripon Road in Tottenham. That was the first place. And we're still in Tottenham now. We moved around, but we're still in Tottenham. It was a real shock when I came here; it took me a long time to get over the shock.

Getting around was all right, because we were not far from the high road. We would catch the 341 and 341a to the high road, to get West Indian food at that shop.

The first house we lived in, there were different people living there, from all over the Caribbean. And the owner of the house was Jamaican. When I came to England, there were already black people living and working here.

How was it when you first came to the UK? Not being able to work? Dad goes to work, living in this tiny little room, and shortly after, you were pregnant and you couldn't work. How was that?

It was hard. And you don't know anywhere really, but I would still go shopping, cook and wash, and take the clothes to the laundry.

Did you have any friends?

There was a lady downstairs who had children. We used to talk and sometimes we would go to the laundry together.

Did you have time to party? Back even when you were in Jamaica and you had no children, did you party then? After Selina was born, did you do house parties?

No, I couldn't! I couldn't leave them on their own. But sometimes I would go to house parties, but not so regular. I had Selina at home. Sometimes they'd give us party invitations, but the party would start at 12 o'clock at night. That's when people should be coming in [home]. So I didn't really do much of that. Until when the children had grown up big. They could stay on their own, so we could go to the house parties sometimes.

I never went to the cinema. Dad wasn't the type to go to the cinema, He would say those things were rubbish. But he liked to go dancing at parties.

Dad loved dancing.

Dad came in 1963 and Mum came in 1964. A year and a half later, daughter and Balford [eldest child] came to join with Mum and Dad. So, it would have been one and a half years after coming here. Then they came and met Selina for the first time. When we first came we were living in Ruskin Road. We moved twice, because we moved from Ruskin Road.

Because when we came, you were at Ruskin Road, and I remember moving to another house in Ruskin Road. I remember you telling me that you lived in Ripon Road, Greyhound Road, and then you moved from there to Elsden Road, which is off Lordship Lane, opposite Bruce Castle Road.

All of those properties were private rented rooms. I never had council housing, because when we moved to Ruskin Road, when you and Balford came, I put my name down, and I didn't get anything. And then we moved from number 2 to 28 Ruskin Road, and then left from Ruskin Road to where I live now. So I moved around the area.

I vividly remember some details about when we came. I remember driving through Fern Gully in Jamaica, which is on the way from St Elizabeth, through to Montego Bay. We went through Holland bamboo. I can't remember who took us to the airport.

It may have been Aunt Reenie?

Yes, I think it may have been Aunt Reenie, and we travelled in one of the buses. And I remember being on the plane, and the stewardess telling us that she would be looking after us, because we were travelling alone. I was six years old and Balford was nine years old. And I do remember feeling a little bit excited. And I can't recall exactly what was going through my head to be totally honest, but I was watching the sun glistening through the top of the bamboos. The next thing I can really remember is coming off the plane wrapped up in this British Airways yellow blanket. It was November, so it was cold at the time, and I was wearing a little summer dress, which came up above the knee, and little shoes.

Oh, I was freezing! We came through customs and sat on our cases, wrapped in a blanket, with the stewardess who stayed with us until our mum and dad came for us, which they did. I mean, I can't recall what my reactions were then, it's just too hazy. I can remember that the houses were close together. Because obviously in the West Indies, the buildings are all in different places, aren't they?

We were travelling by cab, I remember all of that. I mostly remember fragments. So, those were my really early recollections of coming. And, all the mainly white faces. Me and Balford were like [gesturing] sitting on our grips [suitcases] inside the airport, waiting for Mum and Dad to come. [Gloria was nine years old and Beverley was seven when they came].

At that time, we corresponded by letter.

Not that Gunga wouldn't have read them to us.

No, she would just take out what was inside [i.e., money]. No phone calls, just letters. It was joyful, and we were so glad to see Balford and Jenny after all that time.

I just wondered how I would have responded after a year and a half separation, because I was only four and a half years old when they left. My recollection of Mum would have been hazy. Balford would have remembered more.

When I think about disconnection in terms of relationship; I don't really put myself there because I have a good relationship with my mum and my dad, but thinking about it in this moment, what would I have felt? Who would I have thought my dad was? Mum was this lady; would I have remembered her? Oh yeah, these are my parents ... OK, how do I manage that? I was an obedient child, so I would have been compliant in terms of doing as I was told. I wouldn't have shown any friction, in terms of 'you're not my mum, don't tell me...' kind of thing. I was only six years old, so I imagine at that age you just work with what you got.

I prioritised the two eldest children to come first [Balford and Jenny]. To prevent them being sent off to work for somebody or adopted off, because this is what she did to Carlton just after I left. So, that was the most important thing to do at the time.

Gloria would have been four years old, Beverley was two years old, and Carlton would have been ten years old when we left Jamaica. The two small siblings would have been too young to work, and Balford was soon to be ten years old, which was quite a vulnerable time. That would have made Mum quite anxious and worried about what was going to happen to her children.

When I arrived, Selina [her sister] was here. We had no connection when we left, so I cannot remember my emotions in terms of thinking about leaving my two siblings behind. I do know when they finally came it was a shock for them, and us, because they were coming into this family now, where everybody had started to get to know each other. It was new for them, and a particularly difficult time for them, being the two last siblings to come, except for Carlton. They did experience some difficulty, but that would be their story to tell. I imagine it would have been psychologically really hard to be honest, and I would think so, especially for my second youngest sister Beverley.

Beverley had a hard time, and Carlton as well. He took it bad, but at the time I couldn't get him. I look about his passport, but they clamped down on immigration.

Beverley and Gloria came in 1968, and you bought the house in 1968, and they came not too long after. So, as well as saving up to buy the house, Mum was saving up to get the passage, the fares for Beverley and Gloria.

It wasn't easy at all.

I remember little bits and pieces about primary school. There were other black children in the primary school. I went to Lancasterian Primary, and I do remember because obviously I would have had an accent, coming in at that time. I remember my name being mocked quite a lot – Eugenie – and I remember my accent being mocked a lot as well. I met my best friend there, and we're still best friends, all these years later. She was from a similar background. Her parents were from Trinidad, and they lived on Bruce Castle Road. We met when we were nine years old. She came a couple of years later. But there was a family that lived a couple of doors down. Michael, his brother and sister. I think there were three or four of them, and I still see them sometimes. They were at the same school as well. Michael and I were in the same school, and James who's the older one. And I distinctly remember the head teacher talking about James being one of the cleverest boys in the school, and being held up in assembly as being this really, really clever boy. So, I do remember going to school, enjoying it, representing the school at various sports. Throwing the cricket ball was one of them, rounders and even swimming. I don't even know how I managed to get in the team because all I could remember doing was the breaststroke representing the school at swimming.

I think I was lazy when I was young. I know I was bright, but I was also very lazy. But I was not a lazy child that caused problems, so I was under the radar. So, I would always just do enough. I remember when I left Lancasterian, and I went to High Cross Girls' School. I didn't want to go to High Cross Girls' School, I wanted to go to St Katherine's which was a church school. And I remember crying, didn't I, Mum? Because nearly all of my friends were going there, and I wanted to go there. I didn't want to go to High Cross. I went there because it was the next choice. St Katherine's, I couldn't go, but High Cross, I didn't want to go because they had a really bad reputation as a 'pram-pushers' school, because all of the girls would get pregnant. And Mum said, it's not the school is it?

I said, it's the kids and not the school. I said I'm sure thousands of people go there and come out with a good education.

And so, I went there. I love learning, but I was lazy. I wouldn't revise, and I remember having time off to revise. And really remember being in the house, and we had a settee right next to the window.

And I would just lie on that settee and read, nothing to do with study! I would read loads of Mills & Boon books, and even in school I would just be reading them. I got them from the library, because I would spend lots of time in the library. I loved reading and all that sort of stuff.

I joined Coombes Croft Library, which was opposite the Spurs ground. And I would spend most of my Saturdays there, reading things like Black Beauty and all the classic books. I would spend my time reading them. And so, as I got older I started to read Mills & Boon's old romantic books and Barbara Cartland, do you remember that? So, I would spend my time reading, but not studying. I was fairly good, but I just didn't revise, and that was my let-down. I did my exams. I love poetry as well. The first one I really loved was 'Daffodils'. I loved all of that sort of stuff, but I wasn't really focused on it. I loved doing them; it wasn't like I'd sit down and be doing them outside of school. And my mum and dad, because I was a fairly compliant child, they didn't have to say, 'You must do your work, you must do that!' There wasn't anything like that. More with Gary, who's the youngest one, 11 years younger than me. Most of the time he was told to get on with his work.

So, yes, I think I was pretty academically lazy at that point, but I still loved it. I just did enough. I remember doing my CSEs when I was 16. And I got one result which was a top grade, and I got loads of grade 2s, and that was without trying. And then I stayed on an extra year at school and did O levels. And again it was the same thing, because then I got grade Ds in English Literature, Language and Greek Literature; I got all grade Ds again. So I went to Southgate College and I studied to become a secretary. I studied shorthand, commerce, business studies. I did well in that, but again I was still always quite lazy. I did just enough to get something, but not enough to push me.

I don't even consider myself to be British. I don't need to have an accent; what does being a Jamaican mean? I know people who have never travelled to the West Indies, who were born here, yet they sound more Jamaican than I do. I know where I come from, but I don't need to have an accent and I don't have to behave a particular way to be a Jamaican. Although people will say I spent more of my life here, and so I must be English, and I sound English. But I think it is what's inside. I feel that I am more Jamaican than English.

It's how the country makes you feel. The country doesn't necessarily welcome you as a British person. I feel that they definitely don't do that, and so why would I put myself out in that arena. Probably a consequence of my experience of leaving school, trying to go into the workplace, and how that felt for me at the time. It was difficult. I sound the same on the phone, and my name doesn't necessarily suggest difference. But when you get there, it's a different matter.

I remember loads of times being 17 years old, going for work and coming back crying, because you'd go for an interview, you'd get there, and then you wouldn't even get an interview. They would say, 'Oh, you sound different on the phone.' But in those days, 1977/78, it was more blatant. They'd tell you to come, and then when you get there, the job's gone. So, it was growing up until then, different experiences within those jobs.

Although, I think because I was quite amiable, and I could act a certain way when I needed to act, it was kind of like playing the game really. I was not really seen as threatening once I was in the workplace. Although, I didn't stand for nonsense from people in the workplace, and so at times was described as bombastic and difficult.

If there was any conflict really between us and our parents, it was in relation to going out. Especially with my dad. We were not allowed to go out until we were 18 years old and working. Even then my dad didn't want us to go out. And maybe that was the connection with what your gran said: 'Oh, you're going to find man and you might end up pregnant, or there might be trouble.' So we weren't allowed, but we would go out and there would be big arguments on Sunday morning about it because we'd be coming in late.

If Dad said 'No', and I give them time to get in. If I don't hear them come in, I would lay down and not say anything. Because if I say anything, it would start something big. So, when I hear the key in the door, they come in and close the door, then I'm all right.

Apart from that, growing up we were quite compliant children. In the school holidays, at home in Mum's house, we had a great big garden, and we would do things like sing like The Supremes or do Opportunity Knocks, *and do all sorts of things.*

Mum's house is like a town house: it's a flat front and there's about this much before there was a brick wall. And we weren't allowed to go across the brick wall. We could sit on the brick wall, but we weren't allowed to go outside that gate. And we never did, none of us did. Mum and Dad would go to work, but we never did, because somehow we thought that if we did, people would see us and we'd get into trouble. So we never did.

Mum sent me to the shop on one occasion to buy hair oil. Where we used to live there were these bollards on to the high road, and I was jumping over the bollards and broke the hair oil. I was coming home now, with the broken hair oil, and I can't remember the story I told my mum. But she said, 'I know what you were doing! You were jumping over those bollards!' and I'm thinking, 'My God!' In my head I'm saying, 'How did she know that? She must know!' And from then, I thought if I do something, my mum and dad would know, and I would get into trouble. Somebody must have seen me, to tell my mum. In terms of people keeping an eye out for you. That was a big thing then, but I don't think it is so much now because we have fragmented and shrunk within ourselves.

The younger ones coming up now do not care.

I think there was a sense of fear of my dad, because he was very strict. My dad was a difficult person. So, maybe there was a sense of fear of him more than anything. They don't care now if a grown-up speaks to them, or if a policeman speaks to them. I think about that, because their parents would be my age. How come this hasn't been passed on?

I wonder about our West Indian community, the Asian community and the African community, and we look at the different successes that they have, and we think we don't. Maybe because we want more, because actually, I think we have lots of people in our age group who are very, very successful. I don't know what the stats are saying or anything, but I think it's a very small minority of people who do not actually get the wider picture in terms of being negative, causing problems for themselves and the whole community. And then the whole community gets judged. It suits the media's purpose to categorise a whole group of people by the behaviour of a small minority.

My mum and dad never worked in jobs which paid massive amounts of money, but they still managed to save. There's an individual mentality, and we mustn't group everybody together. Mum made sure we got our naturalisation, and it had to be paid for all of us: Gloria, Beverley, Balford and myself. We all got our naturalisation when we needed to get them. I think it's a matter of attitude.

I think some people think, 'Well, we are British, why am I going to pay extra money?' Or maybe they could not afford it.

Some people took a different view. Our view was always that you don't know what's going to happen. Sort it, make sure you have it.

It depends what attitude people had when they were coming. My mum and dad came to work. Not to come and be in the 'motherland'. There are people that have maybe served in the army, and all that sort of stuff. They might have had a different attitude and feelings towards the UK. And maybe that's why I still feel in my heart of hearts that I am Jamaican and not British, although I have spent all my years in the UK. And maybe it is something to do with what your parents filter down to you. For example, their reasons for why they came to the UK.

Sometimes they do these things that people want to see, which is why they wrap themselves in the Union Jack.

If my boys had gotten into athletics, and if they were to become successful, then I would say, OK, they were born and brought up here, so it's different for them. But I could not see myself wrapping myself up in the British flag.

When you go to Jamaica you will find places named Manchester, Liverpool, Cornwall, Middlesex, Surrey; everywhere is bound up in masses of history with the UK. But that history is not acknowledged anywhere really.

I would say, in the West Indies you get better education than here. Jen, you wouldn't remember that. And they gain more discipline!

My dad was very difficult, a strict man. He would more hit [gestures] than talk, although he certainly wasn't one of the worst. He was very helpful around the house etc., but he was very strict. I think people from my generation may have had even worse experiences. There are two theories. So when someone like me leaves home to have my own children, I'm thinking, 'I'm not going to beat my child; maybe I'll treat my child as my friend.' But then, you don't put any boundaries in, and no discipline.

My mum talks about bending the tree while it's young. You don't do any of that. So consequently, you get children that grow up without boundaries and think they can talk to their parents anyhow. So, by the time they get to around ten years old, and they are going to secondary school, and you need to start instilling discipline into them, it's too late because they're your friend. They're not going to listen to you. You have no boundary, you've not instilled certain things in them because you don't want to be too strict, like your parents. I didn't beat my children; I smacked them, but very rarely. I'm not saying whether it works or not. But I think some people went to the extreme, where there was no discipline, and I believe this is the result now. My boys had structure, boundaries and set times to do things. Their dad went with them to football games, they were interacted with, all that sort of stuff. But some people have not invested enough time, and some because they're single parents, some but not all. I know single parents who have very strict boundaries with their children and they're doing very well, thank you very much.

There are some things in certain instances which were left far behind.

The trauma for some of my generation, coming over from the West Indies, being left behind. Maybe not even being as fortunate as we were, to have a mother that thought about the things that could happen to them, and also their experience there, and then their experience here. I know lots of people whose experience when they came here was a very unstable experience in terms of meeting up with their parents and actually ending up in a children's home. So, there was lots of that, which impacts on the community.

I think when we hear about the gangs, they are not just made up of West Indians. There's Africans, Somalians etc., and I remember when I was a legal secretary, doing criminal law, back in those days. We had a lot of black boys who were made up of Africans and West Indians, but when they were stopped by the police, they would all claim to be Jamaicans. And back then, they [the police] didn't know the difference. From my own experience, there's not that many elderly West Indian people still here. I would imagine the demographic now, and I would need to have a look at the census, but it's mostly Africans, from different places in Africa.

Things are still bad, and if the Jamaicans are not coming in, who is doing it?

There is a mix of African and West Indian, or mainly African, when I deal with a lot of the young people at work; young people who have socio-emotional difficulties. So, I think that, yes, there are a small portion, but I don't think it's as big as people make it out to be.

A small few get us highlighted, and everybody's thrown in. There's no differentiation when they speak about what's happening and what's going on with gangs, and there are huge differences. Automatically, when people say black, they assume West Indian, Jamaican predominantly. And sometimes when you look at the names of the people who have been killed or murdered...

In terms of their experience, some of the African countries have gone through lots of trauma themselves. So, the young people coming here also have, or their parents have had, traumas. And maybe they want to leave home straight away because their parents still retain the old ways of dealing with things. There are lots of divisions, but I think it is very much based on, or seen from, the West Indian perspective.

Was it worth it, Mum, coming here?

Yes, it was worth it, for you don't know what your life would be. Britain would be like how it was during the war. For when we came here, there was nothing. There was no money, wages were so cheap, even food was cheap. The people here did not have bathrooms, they had nothing.

Without my mum's generation, I think Britain would be static and miserable, with no lightness. Would the National Health Service be where it is today, if there was no Windrush? What would that look like? And what would the buses and the trains look like if there was no Windrush generation? Things would look different, but there's no acknowledgement of the sort of support and the contribution we've made.

The negativity which is picked up, and fed back to you, makes you feel, well OK, this is what I am, and not this. There's nothing of the goodness and the things people have contributed. I'm not saying we're totally ignored, but maybe more work needs to be done.

I wonder, the 70th anniversary, is that another way of making it look inconsequential? Making it look not worthwhile? Not giving it any sense of importance? So what people remember about Windrush is this, as opposed to the contribution the people have made to this country. I just wonder, why now? And why was it allowed to become so overpowering until the Home Secretary resigns? It's nonsensical.

CHARLIE PHILLIPS

Born in Jamaica in 1944, Roland 'Charlie' Phillips spent much of his childhood with his grandparents before emigrating to Britain in 1956 to join his mum and dad in Notting Hill, west London. Having started out with a Kodak Brownie, for over six decades his photography has captured the black British experience and has graced the V&A, Tate Britain, and the National Portrait Gallery.

Over the years, I documented this area, Notting Hill, and its leading lights, in terms of leading representation of the black community in this country.

We're the only light. Our culture has been overlooked, even by our own people.

It's this generation who are beginning to recognise us. When I had my last exhibition at the National Theatre, people brought their kids to see who their great-grandparents are, as we were coming up to the 70th anniversary of the Windrush. But there's been a missing gap.

Young people were coming up to me and saying, 'Thank you very much Mr Phillips, you're the only one.' That's the only thing that keeps me going.

I always like to start off with what it was like being British growing up in the colonies. I was born in Jamaica in the 1940s. One of the biggest things I can always recall is when the Queen came to Jamaica in 1954 after the coronation. In the village where I was, people would cry, 'The Queen a come! The Queen a come! Our Queen is coming! The Queen a come!' And I always have this flashback, because I lived in the countryside of St Mary which was nice and cool. We were in the Wolf Club, and we thought we knew everything about Britain. 'London Bridge is falling down, falling down, falling down...' Those are the songs we used to sing.

I always remember why I have to include this part of my documentation. I get so excited, because at first they said, 'The Queen is the most beautiful woman in the world.' It's not until later on, when under colonialism, I know what she represents. And we were supposed to be her subjects. That's later on in life. As a seven-year-old... 'The Queen a come! The Queen a come!' I was living with my grandmother and she was so proud when she bought me my cub uniform and my little cub cap. And for weeks we were drilling, 'Left! Right! Left! Right! Stand at ease! The Queen a come! The Queen a come!' Then we used to sing, 'God save our gracious Queen'. When the Queen pass by, you're going to sing 'God save the Queen'.

Now the point is, we had to be getting up at five o'clock in the morning, jumping on this bus to go to Kingston and meet our Queen. It was so hot, I had never been to Kingston before. It was so hot because in the country where I used to live, my granny used to say, 'Come outta di sun! Come outta di sun! Come outta di sun!' to stop me getting dark, and to this day I can't take the sun, but that's another story.

Now, we were in a place called Race Course, where we were supposed to meet the Queen. And everything was delayed, and every minute, 'The Queen a come! The Queen a come! The Queen a come!' Anyway, it was so hot, I remember that day, it was so hot that my granny took me out of the platoon, bought me a snowball, and asked the man to wet the rag and tie four knots in the handkerchief, to put 'pon mi head, and pat mi head, to cool me down. Anyway, when everybody cooled down and got back in line, all of a sudden they handed us these little Union Jack flags, made out of printed paper. The scoutmaster said, 'When the Queen come, shout, "God Save the Queen! God Save the Queen! God Save the Queen!"' Everybody had these paper flags. When she finally arrived, I thought she's gonna stop and say, 'Hello, son, what's your name?' but she just waved! We spent five hours in the morning waiting for the Queen to come you know!!!!??? And she just drove by waving! Seriously, seriously. What does that tell you? No seriously, what does that tell you? How patriotic we were as British subjects. How indoctrinated to be British. No seriously. Nowadays, no pickney would get up at five o'clock in the morning ... well probably not to meet the Queen.

But I was one of those kids because I was so patriotic to be British, so proud to be British, so proud to know we were the mother country. That was my indoctrination against my will, without me thinking.

The indoctrination was the news we got from abroad. I was a Roman Catholic, and father always knows this, and father always knows that, and looking back at it, well that's another subject. How hypocritical it was. I used to go to confession. I did nothing wrong, but I had to make up that I'd done something wrong.

'Bless me Father, for I have sinned.' You see, I was being groomed to be a priest, you know?

Looking back at it, my granny was a diehard Catholic. When I say that, we used to go to church twice on a Sunday, then I had to go to Sunday school, and on Saturday I had to go to confession. It shows you again how indoctrinated you were, that you idolised a European figure.

Looking back 75 years later, how indoctrinated you were! Where they take your mind away and they tell you anything, and you're not supposed to question it. This is where they feed you the bullshit! Through the Church and through the institutions.

After the Queen went, it was so hot. I remember this day very clearly. The driver of the coach decided to take us to the seaside. I'd never seen the sea before. I was a country boy. And outside Kingston harbour was the Royal Yacht *Britannia*, and it look so pretty. I have an inquisitive mind, when di man said, 'It's made out of iron you know,' I sid, 'Then sir… how come a big piece o' iron like that can float like that?'

'I can't tell you that now, son. It can take a long time to explain the law of physics.' But, I was so amazed by this yacht, and ever since then I became fascinated by boats and ships.

Now, four years later, a lot of people were going to England, because they believed in the mother country. 'The mother country needs you to come and help', and looking back at it, I saw people selling their goats, pigs, cows and their land. The land, they used to sell for $5 an acre, to get that £45 passage. The sacrifice we made as British citizens.

We also had a governor-general called Sir Hugh [Mackintosh] Foot at the time. He had to sign our passports. I didn't hold a whole original British passport. I was one of the kids that, when I moved to Kingston, I used to have a lot of arty figures because I used to help people in the marketplace. I was nine or ten years old. I was one of the kids on the waterfront, sometimes diving. There used to be a lot of people selling goods on the waterfront, like souvenirs for when the tourists came in. We used to have a money wall. Because Jamaica at the time was a big centre to the US Atlantic fleet, and there used to be a lot of navy ships, and we used to sell to them.

In 1954, when I came to Kingston, I was so fascinated by the ships that after school I would go down to the docks. The passenger ships would leave from there to take immigrants to England.

Now, this is my first enterprise. They used to say, 'Come here bwoy, you can go buy me a packet o' cigarettes before me go…' I used to run errands for these people. There used to be sweets called 'Mint Balls' and 'Paradise Plum' for the last-minute passengers, you know. They say if you suck the mint ball you won't get seasick. And I used to go and buy Pickapeppa Sauce because they said, 'The food 'pon di boat isn't spicy enough.'

And when the ship started to leave, they would throw coins over, hoping one day they would return back and see Jamaica. I used to be one of the pickney dem who used to dive off the pier, and before the coin hit the bottom, we would grab the coin. This is part of being British for the mother country, your contribution to the mother country of immigrants who have given up their lives and their livelihood. And some of the people who used to sell on the seafront also used to sell in the market. And we used to call them 'higglers'. A lot of the higglers took a liking to me, and because of me brown skin they used to call me 'Reds'. And I still meet up with about four of them; one of them just died, the other day.

In those days, we had to have manners. And, in our community, we had a lot of auntie and uncle figures. I can say I was different from all the kids because I always had an inquisitive mind. But, my little childhood days was to sit on the docks, number one, number two, number three ... to watch the passenger ships coming in and going out. And you would see some bawling: 'Lard, you a go a Englan'! Make sure you drink plenty a' soup, you hear! Mek sure you tek a wash out! Mek sure you tek a wash out, you hear?' That is part of the legacy.

And then the English ships used to come in, like the Royal Mail ship line, and the Pacific Steam Navigation Company, especially the PSNC ships. Most people take a 'wash out' [a laxative cleanse] about a week before leaving for England. The banana boats used to come in and they used to take between 12 and 24 passengers. The banana boat was a bit cheaper. Hence the Spanish and the Italians got into the immigration trade; this was when the fare was £65–75. In those days, looking back at it, a lot of us didn't come here as destitute immigrants, to raise £75 in the 1950s. The sacrifice the people made, to sell their land and their belongings, because they believed so much in the mother country. That hasn't been acknowledged. While they were doing this, people were paying £6–10 to go to all the way to Australia and New Zealand. The historians don't tell you how many people migrated from England to Australia, New Zealand, South Africa, Rhodesia, Kenya. Even last night there was a programme about the Indian migration. After independence, many English people had to come back to England. English migration is even bigger than the black migration. It's not balanced. And this is why I confront some of these people who make these stupid programmes. We have to balance it. Anyway, when my time came to come to England, my father had already come, with my stepmother. He used to send home 15 shillings a month, and we had to survive. As I said, when you mix with a lot of higglers, you can't go hungry. Even though I didn't have a stable diet, for months, I lived on avocado pear and a ting called bulla [ginger cake]. It was fine, because many a times I would get the stale bread from the bakers and carry it down to a fisherman friend of mine. Walking down to Greenwich Park, he'd give me a couple of fish and I'd take them home and roast them.

I was coming to England now, after seeing all these people who had emigrated. And I was so excited as I had never been on a ship before. I was about 11 years old; I was born in 1944 and came to the UK in 1956. I came with two other people who used to live in the same yard, and my half-sister. We came with two other people as kids. And when we lived in Kingston, we lived in a tenement yard. It was a compound, and there would be a communal kitchen and bathroom.

I remember them sen' me the 'landing suit'. The landing suit was a big ting. It was an oversized Burton suit, and a poplin shirt, which you didn't have to iron. You get the outfit about two months before you come in; never wore shoes in my life. When you come to England you have to wear your landing suit. The idea behind the landing suit was to look smart, dapper.

Most of the suits that those guys had were bought in America when they did the farm working. This is why the zoot suit became very popular. You must understand this well, how the fashion changed in England, after our presence. That hasn't been properly documented. But, when you look at some of the archives, we didn't come as no destitute immigrants. The mother country called as far as I'm concerned and we answered. My ticket would have cost £35, because I was a youth, but the average fare was £75. The Chinese travel agency was the main travel service, or we used to travel with Graces.

My parents came in 1955 and I came in 1956. Me and a half-sister came up, and two of our neighbours from the same compound. We travelled together. One of the people was Carmen; we used to play together and she was the same age as me. And this other lady, Mama Seeta. I came up on a ship called *Reina del Pacifico*, which was a British registered ship, part of the Royal Mail line. Royal Mail was a shipping company from England that served Jamaica. They used to bring down all the colonial staff, including the governor-general, and some of the plantation owners. The kids, who used to go to boarding school in England, would be brought to Jamaica with their families on this ship for the summer holidays. A Norwegian shipping company used to run the banana boats, there was the Royal Mail lines, who was a big player, and also Harrison lines which served the Caribbean. Harrison used to serve Barbados and the Eastern Caribbean, and sometimes Jamaica. These are the ships I'd see in the Kingston harbour, as I was growing up as a kid.

I fantasised about going to England, and it did happen.

One of my ambitions was to come to England and be a naval architect, designing ships. Because, even at school in Jamaica, I only used to draw ships and coconut leaves.

I used to sketch a lot of ships, from sailing boats, to steam boats, to banana boats, to passenger ships. There were ships called the SS *Omega*, the SS *Montserrat*, the *Max Caribbean*… There were all these passenger ships. Then later it was the Italians land or the Spanish land; they did a lot of trade. Because people had to get off at Genoa and get the train up. Then Southampton started to open the docks. It was very adventurous. I used to find the nooks and crannies where passengers weren't even allowed. I used to go up and hide in the library and all over, you know? The journey was 21 days. I was enthusiastic, believe you me. We went from Kingston to Havana, and lucky enough we had some friends in Havana, so we spent the day with them, and then we went on to Bermuda and then Nassau.

Then we came to a place in Spain before we went on to France, and then we arrived at Plymouth. We got off at Plymouth, but we could have gone to Liverpool. Then from Plymouth we got the boat train, which was a special train that would unload immigrants straight into Waterloo or Paddington, but I came into Paddington. And there, waiting for me, were my parents.

It wasn't too cold. It was 16 August when I came off at Plymouth, and it was a cloudy day. But when I got up the next morning, I stepped out of the front door and then onto the pavement, and I thought, f****** hell! Is this what England is all about?

I will always remember sharing a room with three strangers. A man used to actually meet people at the station, or if they didn't have somewhere to go, because sometimes the boat train came in late, or due to the weather, or some people had to go to Slough, Staines and Birmingham, and if nobody came to meet them, they'd always come to the house, to find out if the people were staying there. They would pay five shillings a night or something like that, until friends and family come to meet them. In that time there was a guy called Barry Baker, and he used to meet a lot of people. He was the man that met my father and got them somewhere to live. Three of us stayed in the single room that night. It had a double bed and three of us had to share the bed. I always remember that night. Three complete strangers, we slept top and foot down. My parents were in another premises entirely. A double room wasn't vacant at the time. It was not until a couple of days later, when they managed to shift into a basement double room, where all the families slept. We used to have a communal kitchen. This man used to own houses. His name was Leopold. He came over here after the war. He was a policeman and was in the RAF, and he happened to stay after the war. He knew these people coming over, and because of the racism, he knew we wouldn't get places to rent, because it was at the time of 'no Irish, no dogs, no blacks'. So we had to sort out what we could, ourselves. And the English used to say, 'Oh … there's 30 of them in that house!' and some houses had two shifts. So, a group who did the night work would have to sleep in the day, to sleep in the bed, and the same thing at night for the second shift who worked during the day.

There was a lot of slumming, but at least he gave people a roof over their heads. Because no other landlords were willing, and if you didn't pay your rent, you were out. But, if you were happy to slum… We moved around four times before we got somewhere permanent. And I remember when getting a new room, we would carry out rituals. We would get some rum or some whisky and squeeze into the four corners of the room. Then we would light a green candle, get a book, a Bible and a silver tuppence. Because it was alleged that the houses were haunted, after the war. Some of the houses were so damp, you feel the chill and a musty odour. So, my father used to do the ritual and cuss two bad word, 'Come outta di blood claat place!!!' No seriously, we used to bless the house. When you buy your house now, you used to burn the candle with a Bible, Psalm 100, a silver tuppence and burn a green or red candle. Some of the houses had bad spirits. A lot of white people didn't like the black people moving in, so the houses were haunted by white duppy. They said the duppy don't like Psalm 100. I still think that when we bought my last place, we went in and sprinkled the four corners with rum. It's part of the ritual, and part of our culture. I still keep up certain traditions.

Looking back, believe you me, my dad had a business where he employed seven people. He didn't have to come here. But he didn't have business training. The money he made, he used spoil it out, plenty of women around, get drunk, and he was a hustler. He used to make things for the tourists. Crafts was his line of business. He employed seven people, even though they used to get 15 shillings a week; that was good wages in Jamaica. But he didn't have the business acumen. Apart from that, there were a lot of skilled, talented and educated people. From the accountants, lawyers, doctors and engineers. When they first came, they ended up doing menial jobs, because their certificate didn't mean f*** all! Go get a job with London Transport, or the Post Office. That talent and infrastructure that we had all went down the drain. The skills we had were not put to good use.

The audacity of it is that we were all thinking to spend five years. The 'five-year plan'. We became indoctrinated, some of us couldn't advance and some of us were deliberately held back, like myself. Looking back, it was one of the biggest propaganda displays, put on to disrupt the nation, and many families. Even this generation, they hardly have anybody in Jamaica or the Caribbean any more. This is the long-term effect.

Now, here's the new test now. This is when we were known as 'coloured'. Now, I wouldn't knock England, because you have some very nice white people. I remember when I used to get chased by other kids, or Teddy boys, who were older than me, some white women would come and save me. They'd say, 'Leave the little coloured kid alone! You get lost – it ain't fair! Get away from here! Get away from here!' So they're not all bad.

I started going to school, in the September, not long after I arrived. They used to look at you as being primitive. They'd ask me, 'Can you read?' I said, 'Of course I f****** can!' No! Seriously! And there were only three 'coloured' kids in the school. We were now referred to as 'coloured'.

I was at St John's School, Clarendon Road.

So, anyway they used to test you. One of the things I remember is that they would say, 'Oi! Oi! What time is it?' and then they would look up at the sun! They used to think we could look up at the sun and tell the time! Yeah! And another thing they would ask is, 'Is it true you've got a tail?' Yeah! And they would come and rub our skin to see if the colour came off. Then they would feel our hair and say, 'It's like steel wool, innit?' At the time, I had a short back and sides haircut.

First day I went to school, they would refer to me as, 'Nignog!' 'Sambo!' 'Monkey!' Or 'Curly!' There were one or two white kids I would leave alone.

I used to fit in with all of the other kids. And they were surprised that I could read, write, add up, subtract and divide. But here is where the big test come now. I used to have music class, and we would have a big sing-song. 'In Dublin's fair city, where the girls are so pretty…' [Molly Malone].

So, one day the music teacher came to me and asked which songs we used to sing in Jamaica? Some of the songs we used to learn, in the Jamaican private school, was 'Waltzing Matilda' or 'Danny Boy', and 'Oh My Papa' to me was so wonderful. But the teacher didn't know that I was a choirboy in Jamaica. So, the music teacher called me after the music class and said, 'Ron, do you know any Negro spirituals?' and so I said, 'Of course I do!' I always remember that day. She wa'an cry, because of the nice angelic voice; I used to sing alto at the time. So, I sang 'Go Down, Moses (Let My People Go)' by Paul Robeson. I always wanted to be an opera singer. She said, 'What other songs do you know? You sound beautiful!' So she freaked out when I sang 'Ave Maria' in Latin!!! When I used to be an altar boy, I didn't understand a f*** what the songs meant! But I knew the songs by heart. Anyway, at that time, at home, we used to have a Bluespot radiogram. And there was a film which came out called *The Student Prince* with Mario Lanza. And every time they put the record on, I would sing over it. 'I'll walk with God from this day on! I'll walk with God, he'll understand! I'll pray to him, each day to him.' When my parents had gone to work, I'd turn on the Bluespot radiogram and listen to 'Blueberry Hill': 'I found my thrill…' And the white neighbours would say, 'Turn that bleedin' jungle music down! That's all voodoo music is it!!!???' You see how England has changed?

Anyway, I started to develop a passion for opera and jazz. And there used to be a radio station called Radio Luxembourg where the whole family used to listen at seven o'clock. Because in those days they never played music of black origin. But, they had a DJ called Pete Murray, who used to play Little Richard and the Platters: 'Oh yes, I'm the great pretender…'

Now, this is where our family of four would live in a double room. They would put up a little curtain in the middle of di room, and we would sleep on the little fold-up bed, you know? We used to have a communal kitchen on the landing, and those houses that never had bathrooms meant that every Saturday morning we would go down to the public baths to have a bath. And those who needed to do their laundry would do their washing down there.

My little hustlin' at the time was a paper round and I'd go and buy coal for the people. I used to get this disused crap from the coal yard, and then black and white people would ask me to get coal for them. They would then give me a sixpence.

Anyway, I started singing over these tunes. And this music teacher, who was a Dutch woman, said, 'Oh Ronnie! Ronnie! Can you come and sing for me?' She was so fascinated by my voice. She wanted me to sing. 'Waltzing Matilda' and all that. So, she wrote a letter to my father, expressing how talented she thought I was, and wanted me to have music lessons. But my dad said, 'Ras claat mi monkey bwoy ton opera singer!' Ignorant! The first generation without any brains! Because they never believe in us.

By this time the race riots were happening. It was coming up to 1958 and I was an altar boy, at that same church where Kelso Cochrane died. And they wouldn't allow me to be out there. In those days, we would have to put on wired mesh, especially if you were in the basement or on the first floor. We had to cover the front of the building to protect against the bricks and the petrol bombs.

But the main battle took place outside number 9 Blenheim Crescent. There was a guy called Sir Oswald Mosley, who used to keep his meetings out there. This is why I want to get a blue plaque. And one day a whole heap a' black people from Brixton heard about it, and they all came over there. There were two fights outside that building.

Now, just as I'm about to get ready to leave school at age 16, the youth employment officer, who was supposed to find us jobs, asked me, 'Ron, what kind of job do you want to do? What kind of job can I get ya?' So I said, 'I'd love to study naval architecture, and I'd like to start designing soon', And he said, 'What else would you like to do?' and I said, 'I want to be an opera singer, cos my music teacher reckons I got talent!' He goes, 'Ron? Ron? Don't you think you're asking a bit too much? Why don't you get a job on London Transport? Or the Post Office?' No seriously! This is 1959! 'Why don't you get a job on London Transport, or join the RAF. A lot of you coloured people join the RAF, or the Post Office?' We had ignorant parents, who didn't push their kids. That generation didn't push their kids. My folks never read a book in their lives. It's true! I come from a working-class background, and some of the earlier generation didn't believe in education for the kids. 'Go and get yourself a job! You wa'an to be too educated! Go and get yourself a f****** job! And earn a little money bwoy!'

Me and my folks were not close, because they thought I was a nutcase. I was different to other kids. I never kept much company with kids my age group, because I have always had an inquisitive mind. I had older mentors. And the level that I was on at the time, as a 12-, 13-year-old kid, whilst the other kids would be interested in Little Richard and rock 'n' roll I was interested in classics or jazz. I used to listen to Dave Brubeck and I listen to a lot of Thelonious Monk. We had a programme on Voice of America called 'Jazz Hour', and I used to turn it down low while dem asleep. At 11 o'clock every night, I used to tune in to the Bluespot radiogram. 'This is Willis Conover, the Voice of America "Jazz Hour".' And I'd sit down and I fall asleep listening. The beauty of that radio station was, every evening there would be a whole show of Duke Ellington repertoire, and then the next evening would be Thelonious Monk. But my first attraction to jazz was listening to the Voice of America.

Conover did a whole presentation of Benny Goodman, 'Stompin' at the Savoy'. And every evening he would open the show with 'This is Willis Conover, the Voice of America "Jazz Hour".' And he always opened the show with Duke Ellington's 'Take the "A" Train'. As a 12-year-old kid, that's what I was into. Coming from a working-class background, my parents would say, 'You always a' listening to dem mad people music???!!!'

I always say life is a funny thing sometimes, because you don't know what can change you. Somebody could just come into your life and inspire you. I think it has something to do with the frequencies. A kind of hypnotic thing, a frequency where you can communicate. I was different from other kids, and some of my friends I grew up with thought I was eccentric. But, I'm an individual, you know, and I didn't understand it at the time, you know? I didn't know what to do, so I worked in one or two factories, didn't like it, and then I joined the merchant navy, to see if I could have enrolled, but in those days they put you off. You could enrol as an engineering officer or a navigation officer, but I was very interested in the sea and the ships. So, I joined as a galley boy, washing pots and peeling potatoes, just to go on the sea.

In those days, they would fob you off, to make you take a navigational course. But that happen sooner or later and that's another part of my life when Ghana got independence. It was the only country that opened up a lot of opportunities for the diaspora. An uncle figure of mine went and joined the Black Star Line as an engineer, but you couldn't study that in England so you have to go to East Germany to study marine engineering subjects. Especially in technology at the time, they would not allow any black people; they would fob you off when you attempt to go on the course, and it isn't until late 1969 when some African countries started to own their own shipping companies and wanted a bit of the action. My uncle took the chance and went to Ghana and President Kwame Nkrumah paid for scholarships to go and train in East Germany or Israel to learn about either marine engineering or navigation. By the time I was ready to join, dem overthrow the president. But I did about four trips to sea, and found that I couldn't get anywhere because I didn't just want to be washing pots all the time. That's where I feel very bitter. And look 50 years later, Britain doesn't have much of a merchant navy. They never invested in us. In those days, if you wanted to be an officer, or engineer, that opportunity was closed. There are lots of black seafarers who had inspiration, like I did. Not to be just a sailor, but to be navigators, mechanics and engineers etc., but there was no opportunity. I can tell you that for sure. Even with my friend George, who is now sick, we were never on the same ship together, but we had the same interests. And he went on a boat-building course in Southampton. This is where England went wrong. They never invested in us, and they wasted a lot of talent. That's why I have f*** all to celebrate. Look at it now; the British people were not thinking ahead, because they still have this colonial mentality, that they rule the world. It took two other generations to really fuel the change. All right then, there has been a bit of an opening. The other day, I was in a NatWest bank, and at the front, they were all black people. And that's strange, because 50-odd years ago, you would never see that. But they changed too late.

There was an abundance of talent that wasn't given the opportunity and they were being fobbed off because people saw them as subhuman and didn't think they were intelligent.

The merchant navy was something, as a black person, I held very dear to my heart. I thought they would have opened the door, which could have made a complete difference. During the Falklands War, they never had one British merchant ship, apart from the *Queen Mary* at the time, you know? It's sad. We haven't even got a shipbuilding industry any more, and we used to make some good ships, back in the days. I belong to two shipping societies. And we have to go to Hamburg and Rotterdam to look at ships. You come into the pool of London, and there are hardly any British. Something's gone wrong. The biggest shipyard in the world, at the time, had closed down. They just didn't move ahead with the times. I knew something went wrong when I saw that two of the world's biggest cargo container ships had to be built in Korea, partially based on British technology.

With regard to Brexit, they had better stay where they are. Because we don't manufacture anything, we can't compete. They are still living in old colonial times, where they think they are the greatest. The trains don't work, the transport system doesn't work. And you especially notice this when you go abroad and see the efficiency of other systems. We can't compete. I voted to leave, but I think it better we stay and be third-class like the rest of the world.

They never invested in us. Instead, they prefer to criminalise and demoralise us. Ultimately we got a lot of black talent, who are always inspired to do something great, but most of the time they get fobbed off, especially my generation. I can say that without any apology. We were fobbed off.

Photography was only a part of it. But, as I said, I really wanted to be a naval architect. Growing up in London, and living in one room, we only thought we'd spend five years. And so I started taking snapshots and put them in an album, hoping that when we were to return to Jamaica, I could show what life was like in England.

This is how I got my first camera. In those days, there was no entertainment. So we had to make our entertainment on a Saturday night. Those of us who had a basement flat, or a little flat, would keep a little dance and charge two and six to come in. And, in those days, there was a Cold War going on. And during the Cold War era, there was a big United States military presence in England. There were many American airbases. In those days, the entertainment did not cater for us, because we couldn't go to the Lyceum or the Hammersmith Palais, and we were not into the foxtrot or ballroom or Billy Cotton big band. We had to make our own entertainment in the form of shebeens, in the basement flats. The black American GIs were subject to the same prejudices and used to come and hang around with the Afro-Caribbean community, in Notting Hill Gate, Brixton and Peckham. But they used to all congregate in West London, because there was a centre for them called Douglas House in Bayswater. So, some of the black GIs used to come into the shebeens. And they used to find their way around here. All right, a lot of them used to take our women away. And to even pull, we'd have to talk with a Yankee accent. So anyway, this GI got so legless, and he didn't have enough money to get back to the base. And he pulled out this camera to my dad, and

I started using it. Now in those days I was also doing a paper round, and I went to Boots chemist and bought a little book for three and six called *Do-It-Yourself Photography*. The institution do not like when I talk about it, because the first thing I tell them in my talk, is that I did not go to St Martin's School, or Camberwell School, and I don't have a diploma in photography. I'm what you call self-taught. And I learned my trade by buying a DIY book for three and six.

There must be other people in the same position as me. The bullshit they put on you, that you must have a diploma for this. I say, you need to have 'God! Damn! Common! Sense!' I may not have taken the perfect picture, but at least I have documented something, our history.

I was 12 years old when I got the camera and I used to develop my own film in the bathroom when everybody had ga'an bed. I would make postcard shots and sell them for tuppence. And the black people would say, 'You mek me too black man! Lighten it! Lighten up di ting!' If you look at mi early work, they're all grey. I tell people it's part of the culture, and part of the history. Some of those early photographs, people would pay somebody to paint over them. And they're collectors' items. That's a skill.

I went through a lot. I saw the race riots, then Kelso Cochrane died, and I wasn't allowed to go to the service, even though I was an altar boy in that church [St Mark's Church]. My parents wouldn't let me go because of the Teddy boys. They used to roam the streets, with Mosleys, in conjunction with the f****** police! Because the police would see you getting beaten up, and all they would say is, 'Are you all right, son? Just say, "Sticks and stones may break my bones, but names will never hurt me.'" That's the advice we would get from the police. So this is why I don't see anything to celebrate about Windrush. We have been held back, as a people. Even in those days, when you wanted to do good business, and if they see a centre with 20 or 30 black people congregating, all of a sudden they think you're selling drugs. And this is why a lot of businesses of colour never succeed. Because in our own community we used to get fitted up. It was so easy; the police would come and say, 'You can have half a pound weight, or you can have half a gram, the judge won't believe ya.' A lot of black people got criminalised in those days, because of that same behaviour. Now I am doing my research, because I am going to put that exhibition on at number 9 Blenheim Crescent. And also I've been getting interviews from people who were fitted up. You wouldn't believe the amount of stories I'm hearing now. They were so ashamed to talk about it because there was nobody for them to go and complain to.

This is why I told the BBC to f*** off. Because where were you when we were getting beaten up? And where were you when we were being fitted up? A big organisation like you should use your investigative journalism. I said, 'Sorry ... as far as I'm concerned, you lot have done a disservice to our community.' I f****** tell him [a BBC producer] off about it. That's why he never invited me on to his programme. Yeah, I tell him off. I said you have got to put everything in. F*** your paymasters. You gotta tell it as it is. You're not supposed to upset your paymasters, tell it as it is. He run out of f****** stuff. When he first started, he was all right, especially when he did the series on black French soldiers, but he didn't tell everything. He didn't tell how the French opened fire on them when they were supposed to get their pension money. And, over here now, he doesn't touch on the subject of the black soldiers in England who got lynched.

And with Steve McQueen, I had to tell him off as well. He comes around here, wanting to get the hustlers and ponces. And I said that there are more upstanding members in the community. But, when my story came, there were about seven people who got fitted up, and that was one of their biggest regrets. And the last one who told me his story, bless him because he has now died, I won't call any names. But I visited him whilst he was on his deathbed. Because this guy is part of the community. I said to him, 'What is your biggest regret?' and he said, 'My biggest regret is what they done to me Charlie. Dem took seven years away from my life. They accused me of immoral earnings.' Because a lot of white girls used to follow his music, and so he got fitted up. Some of the people from Mangrove, and some of the people my age group, told me how the institution are very good at covering up. And, in those days they'd get a white person to identify, and as far as they are concerned, we all look alike. And some of these people are still walking around free. They should be brought to f****** justice! This man told me on his deathbed. When a man says that on his deathbed, he couldn't be f****** lying. Another one told me how he was planted with an axe, and he could prove it wasn't his, but yet he still got four f****** years. They never tell you how the police used to raid the blues dance, smash up all the equipment and take the f****** drinks away? If I was to tell you that the first person who mugged me was a policeman, when I was coming home from work? He search me:

'What you got there?' I had something like four Guinness. He said, 'Who the f*** you talking to? F*** off.' I have nothing to celebrate about Windrush, until right is being done.

What is happening now is that you have to do things right, and without any apology. A lot of rights have to be done. We couldn't get any finance when we wanted to buy a house. Which is why we had to join the pardner.* And, looking back at it, this generation is the last generation. Because they can't keep the community together, as how it once was. It's like we have a lot of distrust within our own community. We have been indoctrinated, and some of us have bought into it.

Anyway, that's how it started, and over the years, growing up at about 14, 15, 16 years old, I became more radicalised. When I say that, it was part of the alternative culture, which was part of the beat era. I was about the only black beatnik. It was the era of 'ban the bomb' and CND and the Vietnam War. I used to go along and photograph some of these events. I became more politically aware. It was like when the Black Power movement started, even though I wasn't affiliated much with them. I was more or less a radical socialist. Che Guevara was my hero during my revolutionary phases. And then Malcolm X was my hero, when he studied Christianity and what the Church had done. My first photograph that was published was of Malcolm X, in *The Times*. I got £2.50 for it. I felt good about that you know. He was entertaining Dick Gregory.

---

* A popular savings and loans scheme among Caribbean communities. Example: if 10 pardners pay in £10 each week, over the next ten weeks each week a designated banker will pay £100 (the draw) to one pardner. This happens each week until every pardner member has taken part in a draw.

I lost a lot of my archives, and when I used to take them around and show them to the picture editors, they'd look at me and say, 'Did you really take that?' And it's not until about ten years ago they discovered I was black. Most of my work was sold by a white woman. Having said that, it was when I went to Italy that I started to make a name for myself. And then, about ten years ago, they wanted something black to put on. And somebody thought, *'Oh, this photographer's taking a lot of black photographs of Notting Hill.'* And I remember taking my photographs to a curator of one of the so-called institutions. And do you know what he turned around and said? 'Did you really take them?' and he goes, 'Bloody hell, I didn't know that such a community existed!' I said, 'Yeah, I took them because I lived amongst these people. I wasn't commissioned, I took them while I'm good.'

And this is still the stereotype. And nowadays I have nothing to do, because they only call you up when they want something black to put on. So they took me out of retirement because they wanted something for Black History Month, and it's unjust. They were so surprised to see so many people of colour, for the first time, visiting a museum [V&A]. That exhibition was supposed to run for three weeks; it lasted three months. The second time now, this is where I'm f****** pissed off. The second time, they invited me with two other photographers, but I was the main one. There were around 340,000 people coming in. We didn't even have one listing. Same thing in my last exhibition, it wasn't even f****** listed, but it's a good job I have my networking, and my people. Even though they asked me if I could extend it. It wasn't even f****** listed. 'Well, we sent it to all the press people; well, we don't know, you know.'

So, this is it. We still do not have a proper platform, and this is why I do things now, with no apologies. Like, for instance, you know when I came back to England from Italy, with my portfolio, having f****** done work for *Vogue* and *Harper's Bazaar*. 'Oh, thank you very much, it's very nice.' Yet in one of these big galleries, I saw one of my photographs up for sale, and they didn't even say it was mine. Since then, if that gallery asks me, I'd just go there as an observer, and say, 'F*** you.' So, this is what has to be challenged. The people who are supposed to be in charge of the culture for London, England. The other day, there was a programme on about why less people are visiting the museums? It's because you make it a cultural elite, and it's not affordable for working-class people. And plus, open it up to more people of colour, because I'm f****** fed up of going in these places where the only black people you see are the f****** cleaners or the f****** porters. Yet they're a part of London history. When you see that the black girl got the Turner Prize, she kind of apologised in a subtle way, 'We're sorry the diverse community has been overlooked.'

Look at this big cultural event (The Notting Hill Carnival), after six years, you'd think they would embrace it as part of London culture. What other f****** country in the world that attracts two million people for a weekend, for an event, is against it? If this was in New York, they would be all over it; if it was in China, the Chinese would love something like this. But these people are f****** behind the times. These are the people who are supposed to be running our country, running our history, but they haven't kept up with the rest of the f****** world, man. Instead of making something better, don't demoralise the thing. They are lucky they have two million coming out happily and joyful, instead of the bows and arrows and the AK-47s. And all they'll say is, 'Come and join us, have a good time, no hard feelings, we're still here.'

Yeah, but you must include why we were held back deliberately, and now its f****** costing them now, and this is why I personally feel there is f*** all to celebrate.

Some of the white women stuck by black men and they've been left out, which is sad. I always remember this woman, and she used to work in the bakery. Some kids attacked me. 'Oy, you bloody leave him alone,' she shouted out, and chased them away. I feel that if it wasn't for them, I feel that the racism would have been much worse, especially for some of the new generation of mixed-race kids. I do feel that.

We've been held back deliberately, because they saw us as a labour force only, and they didn't realise within our community that we had skilled people. In fact, I see skilled people who can afford to pay their £80 fare, which was a lot of money. We didn't come here as any destitute immigrants. And nothing is recorded of those who spent about three months and went back, or some of them went on to America or Canada for a better life for themselves. In Canada you have black pilots and captains because the opportunity in Canada was open, but we weren't allowed to go to Australia at the time.

When they talk about crime against black people, I personally think it is done through chemical warfare. What they use to distort the mind. And they have a buzz. I believe they have some sort of mass hypnosis on our youths as well, personally. We have to look at life from a scientific point of view.

What are they trying to do? They try to distort it and make it dysfunctional. And they have to do it through drugs and through crime. You've got agent provocateur, and you've got what we don't know about, but we know it exists. Same thing with the Opium Wars in China – that was deliberately done to distort the people. But, the Chinese got it right, because they didn't allow the Europeans inland. Anybody step out of line, just f****** hang them. Because it was used against the population to make it dysfunctional, to limit progress.

They allow a lot of things to go on to discredit us. I came here against my will. And a lot of us came here against our will. But it was worth it from an educational point of view. It opened my mind up to things I had never seen. Who's to say? Because the caretakers who they left behind to organise, they are the ones who have held us back. And they are still the caretakers, because they still have to look after the colonial interests. It was worth it, for the self-education that I had, because I didn't go to university. And it was worth it to survive what we went through. This is why I can go anywhere in the world and survive. I've done it before, I went all over, and I can survive. If you can ride the mental stress they put on you, you can survive. I didn't go to any top university. I'll never get into Oxford or Cambridge. The education I got was of survival, and it was free.

The people who they put through, they never had no long-term plan, and they thought they'd get handouts. This is what they looked forward to, handouts. And they got rid of some of our best talents. And they had nothing to replace them, and that's why we're in a f****** state. As far as I'm concerned, the Caribbean should have been one of the most economical banking places, to trade with people. Which could work if they had a long-term plan. Look at booming Singapore, for instance. Why couldn't it be like that in the Caribbean? Because who they have appointed is to keep the country back. Malaysia as well. Something is wrong. Look at the whole continent of Africa. Every other nationality goes there and does well. The population has been infected, so the mind cannot be developed, and nobody challenges it. And in the Congo they had the sleeping sickness. They tried it on the Chinese and they wouldn't allow the Europeans to go inland, because the population would have been f*****, so they just kept it coastal. In Africa, they went everywhere, poisoned the f****** people, and poisoned the people's minds, so they can never develop. A Caribbean country cannot just run on reggae artists who can sell the country for tourism. And all they can do is kill each other. We need the scientists, and not just reggae f****** artists. A lot of us should be back in the Caribbean trying to develop. When they have nobody to rob, they rob their own. I don't give a shit if you think I am racist.

Our economy has always bowed to other communities. And, it's about time we start bringing back our community. Everybody comes in and take, take, take, and don't give anything back to our community. This also goes for the successful people, who do not give back to the community either. The stars and sports people don't give nothing back, that's why we're in a f****** state.

I don't see anything to celebrate about Windrush, until things are put right.

JIMMY ELLIS

Jimmy Ellis came to Britain from Jamaica in 1963, aged 12. For over 50 years he's built a family, a home, a business and wide social network, but it hasn't all been plain sailing.

Dad wasn't a big man, like me – he was about five foot eight. Right through his life he didn't have an ounce of fat on him. Unlike my generation who drive and eat in excess and all of that kind of stuff, Dad never drove, so he'd walk, he'd walk to the buses and from the bus he'd walk home. So he never had an ounce of fat. But my dad was fortunate that he was fairly well educated for his time. As a result, he believed in education and he wanted nothing but the best education for us. So we, from an early age, would have been steered down that path.

My dad was born in 1922. An only son. He's got two or three sisters. In the Caribbean if you have a son and the son carries the family name, by a kind of hereditary tradition, that boy's important. Look after him, cotton gloves and all that.

What happened was because he was quite a bright lad, and all his mates that I met as I grew up, they're always saying, 'Oh your dad was pretty bright in school', so even though he didn't go on to higher education, the basic education that he had did him fairly well. He dabbled with politics while he was in the Caribbean and he was sort of a political activist, but in those days these things didn't carry violence and all that kind of stuff, unlike today's shooting and killing and all that kind of nonsense. So that's how he was. Then he left Jamaica because his junior half-brother came here in 1957 and realised that it was a bit of a struggle here. His junior half-brother wasn't very well educated so had all sorts of difficulties. He convinced my dad that if he came here, like most Caribbean people came, it was for like a five-year stint.

Yeah, the five-year plan. Get themselves some serious amount of dosh, come back home and do better for themselves. My dad left around March of 1958 and he was meant to be coming back by about '63. By this time, he got here and realised that, you know, the schooling system in Jamaica and places at that time – because we were still under the British rule, because independence hadn't come our way yet, if you were from the middle class you had access to everything, and if you were from the working class you could aspire to it but there were all sorts of financial restrictions in your way – so Dad came here and realised that, you know what, if my wife and children came over to join me it'd be a better bet than me trying to earn and go back.

The five-year plan, from what my dad told me – this is when my dad sat me down and said to me that when he came here, and you hear all about the amount of money you can earn in England, he said that no one ever told him. And he didn't realise this until he came himself, that whatever you do earn – by the time you pay your rent and send some provisions home for your family back in the Caribbean – you've got very little left. So the saving that you think you could save is going further away from it. So he said he came here and the first job he got was at a company called Peek Freans; I think they made biscuits.

And I'll never forget my dad's very first address when he came here, 'cause I used to collect the letters and take them back to Mum from the post office, and it was 15 Camberwell Grove, Camberwell Green, London SE5. I memorised this address, you know, as a little child. When my dad left I was six, you know, so I memorised this thing until I got old enough and drove through Camberwell and saw the road and I had to park up outside and have a look because all sorts of emotions came over me.

Because you know when you're in the Caribbean you picture things … it's almost like going to a Test cricket match and seeing it and listening to a ball-by-ball commentary.

So you've got to picture what's happening, yeah? And that's how it was. My dad said that his very first, um, room that he had rented, he rented a bed within that room. There were three beds of which he rented one. And he said that his rent was one pound, ten shillings a week. Yet his take-home wage was just under five pounds.

He then realised you know what, he'd work as much overtime as he could get to try to build his salary up. So by 1961 he managed to talk to a Jamaican as a pardner, so he choose a pardner scheme and got himself a pool of money and then he bought his first property in 1961. Then by the following year, 1962, my mum came up and joined him. And then he worked up enough money between himself and Mum to send for five of us, so we came up in 1963.

I was 12 when we came. The sister who followed me, two days after our arrival, it was her 11th birthday. And then the brother that followed her, he was born in 1954, so he would have been nine. Then my other brother was born in 1955, so he would have been eight. And my youngest sister, she was five.

When Dad left I was about six, or just past six and a half. So I recall him coming in – because on the morning he was gonna leave, the night before he went out with his colleagues, he came back relatively late and woke us up because he was going to leave early – because at the time we lived about 12 miles outside the capital, so I was born in a place called Brandon Hill in Saint Andrew, and unlike here with public transport where you just go down and jump in a cab, you've got to wait, because the buses might pass at six o'clock and the next one ain't coming till seven o'clock and you have to get to Kingston – because he left from a place called Victoria Pier, which is in Kingston, and he left on a boat called *Begona*. Hahaha ... an Italian boat: B-e-g-o-n-a. All this sort of stuff I kind of romanticised as a child, because that's the only connection I had with my dad, the little conversation. The night before he left he came home and we were in bed; it could have been just after dusk, I don't know [laughs], but we were in bed because children had to go to bed early, that's just the order, as it was. And he came and he woke us up and said, 'Hello, I'm going to be leaving you guys. Whatever you do be good children and don't give your mother too hard a time.' By that time my youngest sister was about four months old, so she only met our father for the first time when she came here.

So these are some of the kinds of sacrifices parents had to make for the greater cause.

We were a very, very close family. As I said, because my dad was very wise in his own way, whenever he wrote – because my mum would get a letter fortnightly – he always used to make mention of all the children by name. Kiss Jimmy for me, kiss Juliet for me. Because of that, when Mum used to come in and say your dad said I should kiss you, we'd get all excited because we felt that although he's not there, he's still thinking of us. Like when an aircraft would fly overhead we'd be shouting, 'Hey Dad, drop some money for us!' and all of that. Hahaha!

As children, you don't even – you know – that's just the way the mind works. When he came, he said, 'Do take care of mother whatever you do', and so on, and, 'Jimmy, you're the eldest, I expect you to be responsible and help to look after your siblings, and don't let anybody bully them', and all this kind of stuff. So then we went back to bed and when we woke up in the morning he was gone. We kind of sat on the veranda thinking, *'Oh God, he's not going to come back!'* It's like a big adventure, but then reality came home. Then come dusk, no Dad. Following day, no Dad. The day after that, no Dad. So then we started asking Mum, 'When is he coming back?' and she said Dad won't be back for five years, and when he comes back things will be a lot better than it currently is. These are the kinds of promises you get.

It wasn't just out the blue, no, no, no. My dad always sat down and he would explain it to us, even though my siblings might not have been old enough to fully understand, and even though I didn't fully understand; all we knew was that Dad is going to go to England. As far as we're concerned, England is like going to heaven [laughs], so that's how it was. So we knew in advance that he was gonna go. He would mention that in a month Dad might be gone, but what's a month to a child? Is that one day, is that two days? Is that 28 or 30 days? So the night before he left when he called us we realised it was now imminent. We woke up and he's gone, and we realised. I had started school prior to him leaving, so I went off to school, and then – that's it. Until he wrote home and said that he was all right.

My first cousin – I was born in June '51, he was born in April '51 and we happened to be in the same class – his father left around about that time. The father came and settled in Birmingham. But his dad came back in 1964. He didn't have the same vision my father had. He came back, decided to go back to hill farming and all of that, and didn't last. He died about '66 or '67 of a heart attack – I don't know if he was pushing himself too hard. I've got some colleagues of mine that live in the Birmingham area now, and some of them, their fathers came – our next-door neighbour, he left about a year and a half, two years after my dad came. When we say next-door neighbour, it's not like a terrace; they would have been maybe, as a child, five minutes' walk away. So there was a trickle effect. I don't think at any one time there was a massive surge. Because for starters, the fee of coming to England back in those days would have been about £55 to £60 one-way, and that is a fair bit of money for people who are getting at the time, like, five shillings a day if you're working as a labourer, which is 25p in modern currency. A day.

So you get five shillings times five, you know … hahaha. To try and get your fares. So that's how it was. Unless you were doing something that was turning over some sort of economy it was tough going. So people came and they'd get themselves a job and would save up and then they would send for their colleague, or their cousin, or their uncle and so forth, and some come and, you know, one help the other and so forth. After they're here and are working for a little while they'd pay them back, because they didn't have the fare themselves. A lot of that went on.

Well from what he told me he had some of the money, and he had a very good schoolmate who used to go and farm in the USA. It's a seasonal thing, so they'd go like for three weeks or a month, or in grapefruit season they'd go and pick grapefruits, and so on. This guy came back and he had enough US dollars to lend my dad some of the money, so after my dad got here and got himself a job then he sent back the money to this guy, you know, so he didn't have the full amount.

From what I learn and understand, back in those days everything – when it was time for the harvest – was all done manually. So there was always a surge, you know, just like all the Europeans come here to pick strawberries?

And when the strawberry season is over, they go. And that's what was happening. So these Americans would come to the Caribbean Basin and get cheap labour. To pay their locals would cost them more. So they come to the Caribbean Basin. So they'll give 'em like a little dormitory in which they live. My uncle, my mother's junior brother, he went to the States back in the late fifties and he did some farm work over there. He said he was in Florida picking oranges and they would have boxes and you'd go up and pick, pick, pick until the box was full; pick, pick, pick and then eventually a tractor would come to pick up the boxes and they're gone. And he said that you could go in a straight line all day, and at the end of the shift, the vehicle picks you up and takes you back to the dormitory. Huge, huge things. But the Americans weren't into having West Indians immigrating, permanently – all you got was like a visa – because they had agencies that would do the work for them in the Caribbean. You'd get like a six-week, eight-week contract whatever the case, so once that's done you're shipped back in, you know? But at the end of the war when there was a massive shortage of labour here, the Brits had a big campaign going in the Caribbean: now that we've won the war, come and help to rebuild the mother country, and get rich while you're at it.

So they were more or less conned, thinking that, well, if I got that kind of money in five years I could come back home and do this and do that. But it didn't quite work out. What you didn't know was that when you come here there were signs saying, 'Room to let: no blacks, no Irish, no dogs'.

My dad said that on the radio that's the kind of language they used. So people got this kind of fervour within their thinking, you know? And so quite a lot of them came.

The British in Jamaica were like the Raj, weren't they? Hahaha! They run things. They control commerce, they control the lot. They control the seat, the government, the lot. Because don't forget only people who owned land and business could vote back in the day, so Marcus Garvey was fighting for the rights of the peasants to get involved. And eventually the British deported him to the USA. Ha!

Threw him out the island, you know. And then when he went over there and became so big and started the Pan-African movement and all of that, then the Americans set him up for fraud. Eventually when he came out of jail, the Brits wouldn't have him in Jamaica, so they sent him here. So that's why he lived there up until he died. He used to be at Speakers' Corner every Sunday morning having his say. Haha! So I personally, from all I can glean, it's that the Brits – because they run the administration and did everything, the head of police, the army, the works – were totally in charge. And the way the system worked at the time, if you were kind of light complexion you could get jobs in the banks and all the rest of it, and if you were a true black man, your portions were less in terms of where you could go in the structure. All that kind of stuff went on.

You knew your place. So it didn't affect you. For instance, I had a white friend that went to the same school as me in Jamaica. When I came here as I said to you, I was 12. Now, they spent like six months a year in Jamaica and six months a year in Bermuda. So they were fairly well-to-do. When they were in Jamaica they had helpers and servants and all of that. But because this kid was really very… he didn't have an ounce of racism in him – his parents might have been different, but his parents were quite happy for us to come and play with him, but we had to play in the yard, we couldn't go beyond the veranda. And you just knew that was your limit: don't go behind the veranda. And the parents would say to us, 'Look, we've got mangoes here, if you want some help yourself, but only from this tree or that tree.' So when you look at it, the more expensive mangoes like the Eastern, the Indians, the Julian and all of that, we couldn't touch, but the common mango you could have. So what did this white kid used to do? Because their fence came to where the drive-in road was, this kid would go and pick some of the expensive mangoes, tuck them up the fence close to the drive-in road and he says, 'Look, when you guys are leaving from outside you can take them.' Hahaha!

When it's time to leave we would tie our shirt and tuck them in from the roadside. If you walk out with them in your hands, the parents would be like, hey, what you doing, put it down!

The thing is, this white kid, I think the only reason why he came to this school is because he didn't permanently live on the island. So they couldn't always get him in – because most white children would go to private schools, and they'd be chauffeur-driven. Because their parents are all well-to-do. I didn't realise there were poor whites until I came here. Because all the whites in Jamaica were wealthy.

Traders and business people, they all had domestic helpers and gardeners and all that. And you, the helper, had to call their children 'Miss' this and 'Mister' that. You couldn't call them Jan, Nick and Jill. You had to give them a title. Missy and all that kind of stuff. That's how it was, you know? But you hear it in conversation, you know, with people you know that work there. That's how it was.

Yeah, I went to a state school. But the school I went to was one of the better-known schools, because we had very good facilities, but they had a teacher training college on the same complex. So, the upper part of the complex was where the teacher training college was, and then we had the school at the lower part. We had our own sports field, athletics track, you name it. Not many schools have them kind of facilities, so that's why we found out some of the Indians and some whites would come there, because it's a good status school.

I certainly didn't have any bad licks in my family. We were smacked if we stepped too far out of line, but my parents never hit us with their hands. They would have a belt, you know? They never smacked our butts or that kind of stuff. Not in our home. Not in our home. But if you overstepped the boundary, you knew what to expect. My mum, she was the disciplinarian. If she was too upset to flog us then she'd wait for our father to come home, and then it would be relief. Because Dad ain't going to smack us. He just sits us down and asks, 'What made you do it? Surely you should know better than that?' And then you'd get a telling-off and you'd feel remorse from being told off. My dad didn't smack. Throughout my life my dad only smacked me twice. It was with a belt, and because I'd gone too far beyond what was acceptable – he's not an abuser – a couple of strikes and he'd say, 'Sit down', and that was it, done.

But the unfortunate thing is that when it comes to that kind of thing across the Caribbean, and I'll be totally honest with you, my island and the people and their mindset and the mentality – violence is accepted at too high a level. The level of violence that is accepted as a norm wouldn't be accepted even in some countries that are at war.

You know how the slaves – Toussaint and those guys – were jealous and revolted? And Napoleon had to go back and get his strong men to put them down? That attitude has always been in Jamaica. That's why in the end, for peace's sake, they gave them land, so we have Maroon towns in Jamaica today. They gave them a run for their money. The Jamaicans were the most rebellious of all the slaves and anyone who wasn't behaving himself was sent to Jamaica [laughs]. So unfortunately, that is something that is probably in the genes.

But then you had lots of little rebellions throughout the island: the Morant Bay rebellion, with Paul Bogle and all of that; we had some rebellions up in Montego Bay, and other places. So there were always things that the British had to put down and keep down. Guys were saying, 'Look, enough is enough.'

It got worse after independence [1962], because of corruption from the guys who took over. So, if your police force is corrupt, then corruption goes down from the top, it filters through. There was a lot more order when the British administration was there. A lot more order. You couldn't bribe their guys. I mean if you commit a traffic offence in Jamaica right now and the police stop you, most of them – maybe five out of ten of them, 50 per cent – would take a bribe. But that's not unique to Jamaica. It's a Third World thing. My observation is that it's a lovely place, I like the place, I could be there tomorrow, but my wife says, 'No, I can't put up with this level of violence.' She says that when she's there she feels caged. She says, 'Why would I leave a place where you've got relative freedom to go and live in a place where you've got to be looking over your shoulder?'

From age nine to age 12 I lived in the capital, with my uncle. Because what happened is after Dad left – you know he left like a farm, an active running farm – my mother couldn't get enough people to pay them to do certain work, so things were going downhill. She spoke with my dad and he said, 'Look, if that's the case, I'll tell you what – there's no point in you staying there if you're not getting the support', because my dad had put things into place and he would send money to pay people and that.

My mum was a full-time housewife. But for the upkeeps and the continuation of the home economy, the farm that my dad had left, he had cousins and other people that he made some plans with, and they would do this and that, and my mum would see to it that they'd get paid, and he would send the money down if it wasn't turning over enough to pay. But there was a lot of envy and all sorts, so people stopped cooperating. In 1961 when my grandfather died, our last support network, my father's father, once he died she just said she ain't gonna stay here no longer. Living in Kingston was my dad's half-brother, and my dad spoke with him and he decided to put an extension on – like a granny annexe – which is where we stayed till my mum came up. Then after that we came up, and that's when I went to school where these white folks were and all that kind of stuff. Because that was in a corporate area.

When I came here it wasn't too long before they saw I was a budding cricket talent and I got sent to Surrey Colts, so I was there at the same time as Derek Underwood and Bob Willis. But because they were grammar school boys they got all the advantage, and me coming from a comprehensive school, only if those guys weren't available I got a game. And the kind of Gentlemen v Players – I wouldn't have been a gentleman because I'm the wrong shade [laughs]. So that was when we went and stayed in the corporate area, until we came [here].

The thing is, the transition from growing up on the farm and coming to England was cushioned by the fact that I went to live in the corporate area. Because once I moved to live in Kingston then all of a sudden you've got fences. If you're playing cricket and the ball goes over the fence, if you don't want to be shot, you go round and knock and ask, or they have some bad dog that will get you [laughs]. So that transition made it easier for me. Leaving the country to go to the town was a bit of a culture shock inasmuch as the openness – and being able to go from A to B, just drift and wander. For instance, as a child if you went into someone's farmland and you were to pick some oranges or something or mangoes or what have you, if they saw you they'd say, 'What you doing here, son?' and you say you've just picked a few mangoes, and they'd say, 'OK, be on your way.' But if they saw you with a bag full of mangoes they'd take them off you, 'cause you're not picking them to eat.

In Kingston, that didn't exist. We couldn't have access to that stuff unless the tree was in your own yard, 'cause you have to clear a fence to get to it. Out in the rural areas there ain't no fence. People just know that the border hangs here and hangs there, and around this little gully is a border, and where that stream is, there's another border. But we had no fence, so you've got no physical constraints. But in Kingston you've got your plots of land and whatever is in your boundary. If some limbs are hanging over the public pathway you might access those, but if you get under a barbed-wire fence to get to it then you're in trouble. You're in trouble. So that transition was made easier for me because I lived in Kingston from 1961 until 1963 when we came up.

When school were on holiday we'd have like matinees, so then it was fairly cheap to go in. We have quite a lot of cinemas in Kingston, and from where I lived to the cinema was no more than maybe half-an-hour walk. Kingston is quite a developed city, but at that time it wasn't a violent city. There was order, as I said. But as soon as the wealth started to move off the plain and into the hills, then urban decay set in. And then violence set in.

You were in a cocoon. Because television didn't get to Jamaica till 1961. Then when the television first came only the wealthy Asians and whites had it. I'm sure wealthy black people had it also, but I didn't know any wealthy black people. So the area and neighbourhood in which you lived limited you to what you saw. You couldn't just say, 'Oh, let's go round Cherry Gardens and see what it looks like.' When school was on holiday – all the little kids – you could only walk around in the daytime. And you're walking along, and they've got these massive Alsatians – you know, keep walking! Because most of these dogs, they're more like guard dogs. Don't try and stroke them [laughs]! But radio we always had, we'd listen to the radio a lot, and on a Friday night they used to have a pop show with all the Top Ten being played. And there was this little comedy act with Miss Lou and Ranny Williams and all that. The first television I saw was another one of my white mate's, 'cause the church we used to attend, the vicar was white, and they were American, and they would allow us. They had scouts and all that sort of stuff, and every now and again they would allow us to come to their home, sit on their veranda and watch TV. So that's how I saw TV until I came to England.

Well, what happened is when my mother left, my half-sister – she was about seven years my senior – became more or less our custodian whilst still under the umbrella of my uncle, which is my dad's half-brother. But my dad was seven years my mum's senior, and he had two daughters prior to … I have and I haven't got a lot of family in Jamaica. The reason I say that is, immediately after we came I was in touch with my cousins who we used to live with. I have one uncle from my mother's side that lived there, and a couple of uncles who were half-brothers of my dad's. Their offspring obviously are first cousins, and we had a reasonable relationship while we were there. But as soon as you travel and come to England then there's like an envy in the camp, 'cause they're fortunate and they're privileged that they've gone to a better place and you've been left behind, and the streets of London are paved with gold and they're sending me nothing. So you get the beggy beggy lecture and all that. So whenever I go to Jamaica and I try to look them up, the first thing that would come up is – like – they think the IMF is in town [laughs]. So after a while I just think, you know what, I'll distance myself from that. I've only got one uncle alive out there now from my mother's side, and all my dad's relatives that were there are all dead. Because if I'm 67 now, you can imagine my aunts and uncles are going to be in their 90s. So I just distanced myself from them. If they know I'm in the city then by the time they find my location I'll be elsewhere. Haha! You know, when my aunts and uncles were alive, a week or so before I returned I'd pop in and see them and give them a change, and some other time the undesirables know I'm around and I'm back in the aircraft. Haha!

It would be nice if we had a relationship with them, but it can't be maintained, because it's always gimme gimme gimme, you know? I went out there once and one of our cousins was saying that he's got a leak in his roof and he's got this, and he's got that, and I said, 'Look, my friend, let me tell you something. I've got a family that's growing up to maintain. Where do you expect me to get that money from?' He thinks that I can go back to England and earn it back by doing this and doing that, and I'm saying, 'My friend, I don't think you grasp that where we live you've got bills to pay, taxes to pay, you know?' And he's saying, 'Oh, but you're here with a wife and three children – look how much money that must cost to come down!' You know, and he's working it out and saying it's $30,000 for the fare, there's five of you – so you're loaded [laughs]!

But they can't see that, they can't see that. So that's why I kind of distanced myself from them, man. And from time to time they call me and want to reverse the charge, and I say, 'You want to talk to me,' you know, 'find some dollars to pay for the call!'

What happened is after Mum left – she left, as I said, I think it was April '62 – and it was February of 1963 that my sister got herself pregnant. And then there was drama.

She was seven years my senior, so she would have been 18. Then my uncle said, 'Well look, if your people in England find this out you're as good as dead.' So they filled her head with a lot of nonsense, and she ran off. So come February 1963 my uncle's wife became our guardian, not out of choice but out of crisis. So my mother decided she wanted to come back to Jamaica to take care of the children. Dad said, 'That's not going to happen any time soon', and then he had to get some funds together and paid for us to come up. So between February and July when we came up it all took time. You have to get your papers, your passport, your photographs – you know, it's a process. You go to the British Embassy to sort this out and sort that out. That's how it went. So we had four months of sheer turbulence, because our uncle's wife didn't particularly want five children on top of her two. Think of the cooking and the washing and all that kind of stuff. So it was turbulent, and my mother was in anxiety because she's thinking that her children are now gonna suffer. The whole idea is that my half-sister would be coming over as soon as they could get the funds together, but the funds never did quite get together before she got pregnant – so we had to borrow funds to make it possible for us all to come up. The problem was that we were underage, so we needed to get an escort. There were lots of complications until my dad managed to locate a friend of his whose wife was coming up – she delayed her arrival by a month so she could escort us. They couldn't have underage children travelling by themselves.

As soon as we knew we were coming to England, it was like a celebration. Excitement, excitement! The way England was painted in the Caribbean is almost like you're one step away from heaven. We were full of excitement. But because of the jealousy thing I was telling you about, we had to keep it hush, hush. If people knew you were about to travel some time they'd get envious and bring violence to you and all sorts of nonsense. So you were told not to tell anyone. And then when we left to come it was during the summer holidays so school wasn't in session, and we left Jamaica on 23 July and arrived here on 24 July 1963. I remember it as if it was yesterday. The old BOAC – British Airways came later [laughs]. BOAC merged with

British European Airways a few years later to become British Airways. We came and our flight left Jamaica, stopped in Nassau, flew on to New York, and then from New York came here.

This was going to be my first time on a plane. From the time my sister left to when my mum and dad said, 'Right, we're going to send for you all, you're gonna come to England', there was a buzz of excitement. So whatever hardship we had to endure, we'd endure it. If there was a disappointment, we had to endure it. Because we knew there was some light at the end of the tunnel. So that's how that was. But in school it was good because we went to a good school. Friends were good, and the genuine friends, they were happy that we were coming to England. They said, 'You must write, you must tell me what it's like,' 'cause nobody know, 'cause unlike today where we've got *Coronation Street* and all of that so you can look into someone, you didn't have that then. It was all just like Test match cricket, like I was saying – you're hearing it and trying to paint a picture yourself. All of that was happy days, that four-month period until we left.

Don't forget, I was young, I had only just done my 11-plus. You didn't have a career in mind yet, because you hadn't quite got to that age. Some people might have done, but in my case, you know. So all you were doing was living day to day under the care of your parents. If you were peckish, your parents would see to it. If your shoe had a hole in it they would see to that. The task of getting yourself a decent education, so you can get in the job market and get a career going, that didn't apply to me. So I didn't have a perspective for that.

It was a massive adventure. People who were looking at the economic climate and this and that, they were probably more the adults of the time or the mid-teens who were looking at what they wanted to do, so I had none of those worries. But certainly, as I said, the lead-up to coming here was full of excitement and buzzing. We were quite popular at school as well – the school dinner lady, we got on really well with her. When we were coming, she came and saw us off at the airport as a friend. She just took a liking to myself and my siblings. I couldn't believe it. So when we came here I wrote to her quite a few times, and after a while I didn't get any answers, so I don't know if she had moved or what, but the trail went cold. There were emotional hang-ups. If you can imagine, I've moved from the so-called country to the city – I've got myself a new group of friends. You had evenings and all your little playtimes and fun stuff that you do at that age, and that was now all going to go by the wayside. That would have been superseded by the excitement of coming to a place that, in your mind, was close to coming to heaven.

Mum was still fresh in our mind as she'd only been gone a year, but Dad was just a letter where your name was mentioned, and he'd answer the letter 'how is so-and-so getting on', but that was the only communication.

When we came off the aircraft – as I was saying we came into Heathrow, and the flight landed in the morning time, and Dad had a driver that came with him – so I was saying to my junior sister, I said, 'That one over there in that red jumper is Dad', and she said, 'How do you know?' and I said that I was sure it was Dad. Because from the photographs he looked the spitting image of his uncle who was always around the yard. You know back in the Caribbean a home is like a complex? So you have a yard, and a man under the tree shading himself from the sun, and my uncle used to live there. And I said, 'He looks so much like my uncle, it's got to be him. I can't see anybody else who'd fit the bill.' My little sister – she was five and a half at the time – was the one that had never met Dad as she was only four months old when he left. I said to her, 'That's him!' We used to refer to him as Papa Coolie. She just ran towards him and my dad said, 'Hey Jimmy', and I says, 'Yes Dad?' and he says, 'Who's this little one?' and I say, 'It's V!' and she just dived onto him. He lifted her up, held her in his arms for a little while – he must have been going through some emotions himself. Now as a parent, if my children are late home I'm having kittens.

I have five children of my own. Four sons and a daughter. So I can just imagine. But on reflection now I'm thinking, boy, he was obviously a tough character, but all of us are human inside there. We then left and his mate came driving the vehicle up from the car park, and we've got all our luggage, and we dump it in the boot and everything else. And then we sat, and in them days there were no seatbelts, so we were standing up [laughs]. 'Sit down boy!' And then as we were driving along I was thinking, there are so many factories here in England because we saw all these chimneys! Dad was saying, 'Ah, this is the road I live on now', it was near The Oval, it was a road called Mostyn Road which comes off Brixton Road.

So the second road on the left, Bramah Road, coming in from Brixton Road, is where my dad lived – number 37. So when we got there and I'm looking around and I'm saying, 'Is this the road you live at?' and he said, 'Yeah', and I said, 'Well, how come the house is so big and so long?' and he said, 'No, no, no son. Just this one storey is mine, all the rest is different numbers.' But I couldn't get my brains around it, because I'd never seen a terraced house before. But then when we moved in, and Mum was there and she was all excited – and she started to cry when the entrance door was opened – and she was sitting at the bottom of the stairs, and she mopped up all her tears and she came and hugged us, embraced us. And then when we sat down and Dad started to ask this and ask that, we heard someone crying, and we said, 'Who's that crying?' and she says, 'Oh, I've had a baby.' So by the time we got here, we had a two-month-old sister, the first of the red, white and blue! Hahaha!

So that kind of came as an attraction and a distraction – everything wrapped up in one! The excitement of coming home and Mum saying, 'You guys must be hungry', because the aeroplane food was just – you know, bread this and bread that – so Mum went and rigged up some breakfast for us with bacon and beans and hard dough bread and all the sort of stuff that we were used to. And then we sat down and Dad started to ask how we were getting on in school and all this and all that. Because Dad, everything about him was all education. Whereas Mum was saying, 'Let the kids have a second to relax for a little while.' I was looking around and I was saying, 'But Dad, it's not cold here', and he was saying, 'No, no it's not cold,' because they were telling me in Jamaica that England's so cold that it's like in a fridge! He was saying no, not this time of year. He says, 'We have the four seasons, but when winter come you'll see.' Because we came here on 23 July and it was a lovely summer, and I'm saying, 'Oh, they've got trees in England!' because in your mind you conjure up all sorts of images. Hahaha!

The first day here, even though we had a little bit of jet lag – when we got here in the morning, it would've been like 2:00am or 3:00am in Jamaica – so it wasn't too long after we'd had something to eat that we were all kind of sleepy. Then we woke back up and Dad told us he'd taken the day off work, so he wanted to walk around and show us the park. We had a park called Slade Gardens, and one called Myatt's Fields that was just behind the school that I went to, near Kennington School. So he walked us around and showed us around, and the first thing that was a shock to me was the fact that everything you did in England was all indoors. Whereas back in the Caribbean, you go indoors only when it's time to sleep or time to eat. So that was the first thing that I had to try and get used to. And Dad would say to us, 'Well look, this isn't Jamaica, you've got to have a different attitude to the roads; the roads are very much busier. I don't want any of you guys riding bicycles, the roads are too dangerous and I don't want any harm to come to you guys.' So he had to sit us down and lay down the rules – father lays down the law, mother's supposed to enforce it [laughs]. That's how it was. And because we came at the start of the school holidays, it wasn't until September that we actually went to school.

My very first experience of the white folks around me was how difficult it was to understand them. I could understand the newscasters, because they'd speak in kind of … Queen's English. But the guys in the street, that was a bit of a struggle. Because they're speaking and they're abbreviating with a touch of Cockney, so it was a struggle. I'll never forget the second day we were here – because Dad had taken us round to where the post office was on a road called Ackerman

Road, and they had a paper shop there where they sold lollies – Dad gave me some money, and I went round and I thought that I'd just buy one of these ice pops. So I asked the man, I said, 'Can I have one of those, please?' Because Mum said whatever you do, always say 'please', and if people don't understand you, just say pardon then you repeat yourself. I went round there by myself, because the rest were back at home. And I bought this ice pop, and the lady said, 'Three apes, son.' And I said, 'Pardon?' She said, 'Three apes.' I said pardon a second time, and she said, 'Three apes.' So, I scratched my head and went in my pocket, took out all the money I had, and then she took a penny ha'penny in old money [three ha'pence], and I said 'Ah!' So I thought, right, when I went back home I could start to educate my siblings now.

So now I'm saying that three apes mean a quattie [a quarter of six old pence]. We have a song in Jamaica we used to sing, 'I carry me ackee, go a Linstead Market, not a quattie worth sell.' Because that's what quattie was. Every opportunity I had to learn a new word, and how they say things, I'd then educate my siblings, but by the time we got to school I could hardly understand the white kids. Because I was just one of three black kids in my class, and when it was time for play, that's when the depression started to set in. Only now can I equate it to depression, because at the time I didn't know what it was. The thought now of me in the playground – because back in Jamaica you go and play cricket, you know? It's not 11-a-side, it's one man bats and everybody fields, so you all get a go. And if you're playing football and it's 11-a-side, topless and tops on – that's how you separate yourself, so everybody got a look-in. But these guys now, they didn't know you, so they didn't offer you a game. So you just stood and watched. And there wasn't enough of us to get a game of our own going. So when it was break time you learned the routine, the ringing of the bell, and the line-up so you can go back in, and back in those days they used to issue milk. And they used to have doughnuts you could buy, and the doughnuts were like a penny, or maybe two pence, so our parents would give us some money and we had some of that at break time. And at lunchtime, again eating the bland food which the British cooked, it was a struggle; compared to what we were used to.

And we're not used to it, because coming from the Caribbean – you know – we need something flavoursome! And then cheddar … none of that kind of stuff. So effectively it was a gradual thing. But then the first shock that I had was again in the playground, when this white guy called me a 'wog'. This was my first experience of overt racism. This was when I went to school. Because when we were in the school holidays, we were just playing amongst ourselves, weren't mixing with the community per se. In the school, I remember his name, this kid, it was Colin Flood – I'll never forget him – he called me a wog, but because I didn't know what a wog was, I just kind of went quiet. And then when I went home and I told my parents they said, 'Ah, they're just ignorant. Ignore them.'

That happened within the first week. So after a while you just kind of go into your shell, because all I was trying to do was to try and make friends, because I wanted to get involved and play, like any other child wanted to play, you know? To be called a wog – it was a bit, you know – that was a shocker. Absolute shocker. And then it became a regular thing that we just had to kind of link up with each other and keep our little combination within our community. I don't know about my siblings, but I certainly was the only one who went on to secondary school because of my age; the others went into primary school. So I had the responsibility now of trying to shield them – and once I learned what these words meant, then I would just go and explain that if anyone calls you that it's not very nice, so let me know and I'll come round and fat up their lip [laughs]. Coming from the Caribbean that's all you know! If someone mess with you, you just have to get violent. This is why we have this reputation for being violent. It was kind of forced on us. We didn't come here to try and fight our way about – it was survival, innit?

After the Jamaicans, the Bajans were probably the next biggest group. Those early Bajans had their fares paid, 'cause they came here to drive the buses. The Bajan licence to this day is valid here in England. So Bajans coming here, if they've got a Bajan licence, they don't have to retake their test. Same with the Kenyan and the South African licence, which is valid here. So these guys came and drove London transport.

My parents found out where – because they had various places where you could go and buy the uniform, you know – so I had my jumper that we didn't need in the summer, and my blazer and all of that. The very first day, I can't forget it, the headmaster – a man called Mr Fawcett – he sat me down and said, 'Right, where are you from?' and I say, 'Oh, Jamaica', and he says, 'All right. Here's a book, read that.' And I read, like, a chapter of the book and he said, 'OK, fine', and that was it. But because I had passed the scholarship in the Caribbean before I came here, which is the equivalent of the 11-plus, I thought that would have been brought up at the interview stage, so they realised that I'm not just the average idiot. But in the end, it didn't. So, after about three months of me doing vulgar fractions and all that kind of nonsense, I sat down next to Dad and said, 'Look Dad, the stuff I'm doing at school is a waste of my time, because I covered this two years ago in the Caribbean', so Dad said, 'OK, don't worry.' He made an appointment, went and saw the headmaster, the guy sat me down and we had a good chat, and then I got put up into the higher graded classes. So then I started to do some challenging stuff. But the first day, as I said, just the layout and everything was so different from what we were used to in the Caribbean. The entire playground was tarmacked, with big high fences – so we had a high wall, and then some meshing on top of that, not barbed wire, but meshing, so you couldn't scale it. Once you're in there and the gates are locked, you know you're in [laughs]. And that was the first thing that really caught my attention: that if we go swimming, we'll be within the four walls. If they took us to the indoor nets, we're within the four walls. If we're in the playground, we're within the perimeter of the walls. It was almost like a prison in a way for me. So it took some adjusting. On top of that, you've got people who don't know you and don't want to know you, and call you all sorts of names and get the worst out of you. This same kid, Colin Flood, who called me a wog – once I knew that wog wasn't a good word – the next time it came out of his mouth, it's like bust his nose and neck, innit. Then I got into trouble and the teachers called me. I can't remember if I got detention or if I got caned –

back in those days you'd get caned – can't quite remember whether it was the cane or a detention. But I bust him up, man. So now we would start to get a bit of a reputation, because the anger came from nobody wanting to know, from nobody wanting to hear your point of view. So you were just on the outside looking in.

It's not even like you want to fight, but that's the only way you can get the frustration out. Because they're talking to you in a language you don't fully understand, and they don't want to understand you. Coming from the Caribbean, our English was reasonable, but because everything they spoke was abbreviated with the Cockney and the accent and everything thrown in, we basically couldn't understand each other in the early days. By the time I started to catch on and learn a little of what they're saying, by the time I was in school for, say, five or six months, I could understand enough. So the new black guys coming into the school, when the white youths would speak to them and they couldn't understand, they'd come up to me and say, 'Hey Jimmy, what's that?' and I would be the interpreter [laughs]. Yeah, I became the interpreter and would tell them what was going on, till eventually they caught on a little bit, and so on. It didn't take long because some of what they're saying you understood and some you didn't. But if you don't understand the full sentence then you don't necessarily know exactly what they're saying. So that's how it was in the early days, until such time when the first winter came.

We were fortunate. There was a severe winter that took place in '61 or '62; lots of people lost their lives and all sorts. When we came, the winter of '63 was quite severe, but not as much snow settling on the ground. But it was pretty cold. Because even back in those days, parts of the Thames would freeze over, and the ponds in the park would freeze over. I remember going shopping with Mum – because Dad didn't have a car we'd walk from where we lived, just off Ackerman Road. We'd walk down through Burton Road and then go to Brixton and go shop – but in those days, carrier bags were like paper bags with a little kind of cord. I'll never forget we came home the Saturday morning, and my mum had one of those push baskets. And myself and my sister and one of my brothers went shopping. And when we got home, Mum opened the door and we went in, and when I put the bags down my fingers wouldn't straighten. They were so cold that they were still in this position. And I foolishly made the error, because we had these paraffin heaters for warming the place – not like today with the central heating and all that kind of stuff – the fumes were enough to blow you up! I went in and put my hand around it to warm my hand up, and it started to sting, and it was so painful I started to cry. Because it was just the frustration of not quite settling into this new place, not being accepted by the people around you. If you were lost and you asked an adult where to find such-and-such, maybe one in five adults might answer you. Four out of five would just look at you as if you didn't exist and walk on.

Sometimes, especially in the winter months, everywhere looked alike when you first came here. So unless you've got some landmarks fixed, you'd be a bit lost [laughs]. Once I get to Ackerman Road I know how to find my way. I remember saying to my dad, 'I want to go back to Jamaica; I can't handle this. It's too cold.' And he said, 'Come here, Jimmy', so I went into the lounge, and he said, 'Sit down right there, son. The next time you go to Jamaica, it's your money that's going to take you there, not mine.' And then the harsh reality came over to me that, do you know what Jimmy, you're here to stay. I could not believe how cold it was. But then after that Mum advised me never to put my hand close to the heater again. If ever my hands are that badly frozen then the thing to do is just give it half an hour once I'm inside and then it'll thaw naturally. But it was painful, man, very painful, I'll never forget that.

Back in those days you put stuff out, like we just put a mug of water on the windowsill, and we come back in the morning and it's frozen solid. And I used to write to my mates in Jamaica and say, 'Wow, this thing called winter just come [laughs]. And it's colder than a fridge, don't listen to what they tell you!' It was bitterly cold, bitterly cold. But you know what, by the next year I'd got accustomed to the place. And then I made a new group of friends, mainly blacks, with the odd white person who lived local and would say hi, and things started to settle. But the grown adults, they were kind of still ignorant to who we were, saying, 'Why don't you go back to your jungle!' and stuff like that. You'd get that comment on a regular basis. It might not be every day, but it seems like every day.

Well this is when I became a little bit militant. Prior to that, I will never forget that we had a schoolteacher called Mr Kay – he did maths, but he wasn't very good at it. I'd say, 'Oh, I don't quite understand that, sir', and he'd go, 'Blah, blah, blah!' and move on. But if ever the white kids didn't understand anything and put their hands up, he would then go next to them and help them to resolve it. But he would never come next to one of us lads. He'd stay at the blackboard and discuss it. So straight away I started to think, 'Hmmm.' Because racism wasn't even a word to me then. As I got older, I understood it, and I realised that he had a problem with black people. He wouldn't come close to us, but he'd go next to the white kids and explain the maths. But with myself or any other black kid, that's how it was. He'd blabber from where he was and never come next to us. I'd go and sit down and talk to my dad about this and he'd go, 'Look, son. As long as you're in this country, a handful of these people will be ignorant. You just know what you know, do what you have to do and get on. If you get yourself an education – they can take away property, anything, take away your car, your clothes – but they can't take back the education. Whatever part of the world you go, if you're educated you will stand a better chance of surviving than if you're not.' So that was his ethos.

Thing is I was an obedient child. If Dad said so, then so it was. The only time when I would start to think differently and wonder if Dad's right was when I came into my mid-teens and started to form my own opinion. But as a child I just did as I was told.

Mum started to work in 1964, so by that time I was 13. She had a year out after the birth of my first English sister, and then they sat us down and said, 'Look, if you guys are going to have the things you need and have a better quality of life, then Mum's got to go into the work environment. And so you guys are going to have to help out the best you can. And it was my job to take my junior sister to the childminder and to pick her up in the evening. So if my mates stayed back playing football and all that, or cricket, I'd have to leave. At ten past four school was over, and by half past four I'd have to pick her up and get her home, and then Mum would be home from work at about six o'clock. My dad mainly worked nights, so he would disappear about 6:30pm or 7:00pm, and he would come home in the mornings at about 7:00am or 7:30am.

The thing is I was searching for consciousness. Because the school system never taught me about me. It taught me about Marco Polo, Captain Morgan and all these people that never taught me about me. So I was on a quest to find out who I was culturally? The music on the radio didn't reflect me. The programmes I'd see on television didn't reflect my lifestyle. So am I an alien? Who am I? So that quest started. And it so happened that we had an Olympics in Mexico, 1968. Tommie Smith, John Carlos, Black Power, the struggles – all of a sudden, most of us conscious black youth started going into the Black Power ideology and trying to find ourselves. The struggle was going on in America at the time. By this time, they had taken Muhammad Ali's title off him because he refused to fight in Vietnam. He said, 'My fight is here in America. Because you are the guys calling me "nigger". The Viet Cong never called me that, so why would I want to fight them?' So that level of consciousness – all of a sudden, we're thinking, yeah, this is the struggle we now need. And that's when my little bit of militancy came on. So I then started to go to Black Power meetings and listen to all that was going on, and some of my mates then decided they wanted to become Rasta men. There were two strands – either you start to burn the herbs and stuff or you had your big Afro styling [laughs]. So that's when I started to think to myself, you know what, them people have made us captives, and they've done this to us and they've done that to us, and now they are denying us. By this time I had now started an apprenticeship, and I went into manufacturing.

I left school at 17; I stayed on an extra year and did my A levels. Then I went on – because back in those days an apprenticeship was very popular – so you'd do what they called a sandwich course, which was like three months in college and three months in the workplace. So I was in the process of doing all of that while still studying. Then I realised that there were barriers within manufacturing. As a black person, they only allow you so far within the management structure, and doors are shut in your face after that. So once these things start to become clear to me, I now start to say to siblings, 'Think of the career you want to go into.' Because if you go into some of these various things like I have found myself, spent all this time doing my apprenticeship and all my studies, to find that I cannot break into the management structure because that is for the whites only – this is what I was up against.

So all of that added not just to the anxieties of the world, but to the tension and the frustration and helped to make me even more militant. So I then started to get involved with the Black Power movement and things. I'll never forget – I was going out with a Bajan girl – and once her parents found out I was Jamaican, they didn't want her to go out with me any more. Because they had a thing called the West Indian Federation, which was before CARICOM [the Caribbean Community], and when that fell apart the Jamaicans got the blame for it. I'll never forget, I went to this dance at Oval House, just across the road from The Oval cricket ground. Before the dance started, I've forgotten the name of the guy – Dr Carmichael? He wasn't there, but he had his sort of cohorts there to educate the masses – so this guy did this little thing and we were saying, 'Yeah!'

and then all of a sudden, the police wanted to come and break up the thing. So the police claim that some kids mugged a lady at the Oval underground station and came into the dance, because they wanted to pursue them. The guys who were holding this thing say look, as far as we're concerned, all the people in here have paid to come in, so if you want to come in you have to pay [laughs]. So the police disappeared, and about ten or 15 minutes later there are police with Alsatian dogs and a battering ram and everything, and they let the dogs go and women were screaming, people were being beaten, so I had to grab hold of my girlfriend and I left through the fire exit. Fortunately, I didn't get cut or anything, and then they locked up the other guys, and what they did was they dismantled the Black Power Movement bit by bit. They did it kind of covertly, you know? And in prison these guys trump up charges and all sorts of nonsense. Then the 'sus' law came in. So you stand at a bus stop waiting to take a bus and the police would come and lock you up, saying that they suspect you were standing there to mug an old lady. All that kind of nonsense. So you can understand now when we went to, like, the carnival, after dark there was an opportunity to throw two bricks at a police car – because these guys were unreasonable. Eventually I said to myself, enough is enough, I'm going to vacate this place. So I started looking at emigrating to Canada. I started looking – because I was in manufacturing – to see if I could get into California's Silicon Valley, so I contacted the various services and was in the process of filling this in and filling that in, and my dad sat me down and said, 'Wherever you go, if the guys who call the shots happen to be white, you're still going to be up against it. So it might be in your best interest to stay here and fight rather than go abroad, because all you will do is be in a place where you've got no friends, no family, no back-up, and you'll still have the struggle on your hands.' So with that I thought, you know what, maybe Dad's got a point. So I stayed here and worked my way through, got some fairly decent jobs. At the same time every time I got to a place where I realised there were barriers in my way, I'd find myself a new job, get to as far as I could go and find there are new barriers in my way, and it went on. The system was constantly against us. But in doing what they did to us, two things came out of it: our parents' generation, because they couldn't get council apartments, they build their own. And a lot of them became property millionaires. And then the second thing was that the others who didn't excel and stayed in council estates, unfortunately they are producing today's thugs.

It's a generational thing. Our parents' generation believed that we should obey the law and the law is right. I had sat down with my dad and said, 'Some of my schoolmates, the police have planted drugs on them and ruined their future. Drugs are something I would never touch. If ever the police were to come to this home and say that I was found with drugs, you're going to have to remortgage your home to defend me, because that's something I would never do.' Walking around with knives and drinking excesses of alcohol, that wasn't me, and it never has been. So my dad said, 'Son, I'm glad you're bringing this to me. In this country, the police – what they say and what they do isn't always the same. And as long as you are honest with me, I'll do whatever I have to do to defend you.' I've never ever been planted by the police. I've been harassed, I've been stopped, I've been pushed around and dragged out of a car; all sorts of nonsense. But never did they set me up like that.

But my parents, they were shielded from that, because they would go from work to home to church. They weren't going to no cinema, they weren't going to no nightclub. They're not going somewhere to play a game of football or a game of cricket. So because they just go from A to B, and from B to C, they were literally not exposed to some of these experiences that we've had. But we were young and full of energy, and I wanted to play sports. I wanted to go here and go there. I wanted to go to the cinema, I wanted to go skating. But whenever you go out in public like that it means you've got to use the road. A classic example is going to All Nations nightclub in Dalston.

I picked up my mates and we got to Elephant and Castle but got stopped by the police. 'Your car?' I said, 'Yeah.' He said, 'Where did you nick it?' I said, 'Brixton Police Station, now nick me.' 'Out the car!' You know, they pulled me out the car, went to search it and all the rest of it, but couldn't find anything wrong with the car, but gave me a 'producer'.* So we went on to our rave, left All Nations about four in the morning, maybe three or four-ish, got to London Bridge, got stopped by the police again. By this time I'm not cooperating no more, I've had enough. My mate in the back seat says, 'Look, we got stopped about five or six hours ago, officer.' And he's had enough. So he took the 'producer' out of the glove compartment, gave it to the police, they saw that it was dated on time and said, 'All right, be on

---

* An HORT1 ticket issued under the Road Traffic Act 1988. It requires a driver to produce their driving documents to a police station within seven days of being stopped by the police.

your way.' And at that point I got to a place where I was almost fearful to drive a car around.

I'm probably about 22, 23. Maybe 21, 22, something like that. But what I have found out, and this is why I sat down and passed the information on to my siblings and my children, is that every time you've got your car full of your mates, you're likely to be stopped, whether you're black, white or Asian. Yet if you've got a car full of women, or you and your girlfriend, they ain't stopping you. So once I've got the experience I pass it on. I said, 'If you don't want to be stopped, have a car full of women or your girlfriend. But if it's you and your mates, expect to be stopped.'

With my wife – I met her when I was 22, and then we started dating – we never really got stopped. I got stopped maybe once, possibly maybe twice when I was going out with her. Police would come up to the traffic light, look over, and if they see you with your girlfriend, it's go back to business. But if you got two mates in the back, one in the front, nee-naw, nee-naw!

My dad wouldn't know where a nightclub was in this country when he was alive, nor would my mum. My mum was a Christian all her days, so she wasn't a going-out person. My dad wasn't a pub person. So it only happened when him and his mates got together and they played some dominoes, drink two Guinness, cook some curry or something [laughs]. That was their entertainment. So they didn't have to kind of interact with the general public like we did.

I think I realised that I was here to stay … when my first son was born, because my first two children were prior to me getting married. When my first son was born, suddenly it dawned on me that if this kid is going to eat, sleep and drink, it's down to me. And that kind of grew me up. So I decided, you know, that I'm going to dig in, and that I'm going to fight. And whatever I need to do to make ends meet, and to make sure he has a better life than I had, I will do. So rather than have a chip on my shoulder I started to think to myself, you know what, I have to fight the system somehow. I went through quite a lot of jobs, basically because as soon as I realised that it was a dead end and that the promises made at the interview are not going to be fulfilled, I'd find another job. But then the point came in the late seventies, early eighties, when Maggie decided she was going to decimate manufacturing and most of the manufacturers based within the M25 belt moved out. Then I got job offers in places. But I thought to myself, the nonsense that I had to put up with in the sixties because I was a so-called ethnic minority, I don't want to expose my children to that. And now that the big metropolis as it stands is multi-cultural, multi-ethnic, I want to leave my children within that kind of belt so that job opportunities will be better for them. So I just stood my ground. Around about when I was 21 or 22, I came to the conclusion that I'd dig in and do what you have to do. Fight the system and do what you have to do. I became a victim of my own tenacity, because I wanted to offer my children more than I got. And in doing so, I did work in manufacturing, and that's how the driving school got started. I decided in my spare time I would do some additional work so that they could have holidays and school trips and skiing holidays and all that. My son was quite bright and went to grammar school. They'd go on tours to the Caribbean and play cricket, which I'd have to pay out my pocket. Rugby tours to

Canada and America. And I'm thinking, whatever I do for one child, I've got to be prepared to do for all of them. I did what I had to do to get my five through the system.

I started the driving school as a way to make additional funds. But it meant that I was working in manufacturing in the daylight hours, and in the evenings and weekends I would do a bit with the school. It got fairly successful, so then I employed some people to come on and offered them a full-time job and I took a back seat. Until 1999 – that was the last year that I worked in manufacturing. I was working from out of Hemel Hempstead, but the commute, you know, coming down the M25 was 62 miles each way. So I thought to myself you know what, enough is enough. So come 2000 I started working full-time in this thing, and boom boom.

If I'm being 101 per cent honest, I'm 100 per cent Jamaican and I will always be. Will I ever live in Jamaica again? The answer is no. But Jamaica has always been home and will always be home, 'cause when I'm there I feel part of it. And I think this is where I well and truly belong. But in all practical terms because of the level of violence that is accepted in that society, as you get older you're less capable of looking after yourself. So logic tells me that if I was ten or 15 years younger and I could probably stand up and fend for myself, I could probably live in amongst them. But it's not going to happen. Even if I wanted to do it, my wife decided that she loves Jamaica but don't like Jamaicans!

She is Jamaican by birth herself you know; if she was not Jamaican and said that to me I would be offended! Hahahaha! I mean I've got land and stuff out there still, and eventually with that part of my estate, my children can do what they want to there. But my dad always said to me that if you've got land in Jamaica, it's worth holding on to. Because these Europeans, they can't stay peaceful for very long. You never know when all sorts of bombs are flying, and if you've got a safe sanctuary you can retreat to until the fireworks are all over, it's worth holding on to. So for that reason I do think Dad has got a point, he's got a point.

Right, now, faith came about – 24 years ago. When I lost my father, he died quite young; he was 56 when he bowed out, cancer of the liver. Dad was always in the picture somewhere, and then when we came here, Dad was influential. When I was militant, Dad said he understood the way I feel. So Dad always had a calming influence on me. And I saw Dad as this – I don't want this to sound in a derogatory way, but he was more like a stable black man who took care of his children. The unfortunate thing about people who are the by-product of slavery is that we love to hit and run, and we don't stand our ground and take care of the children. So when he bowed out at such a young age I thought to myself, there ain't no justice in this life. He's always been there, and as long as I've known him he's working. And I often said to him, Dad, when do you get time to do this and that? And he said I'll tell you something – when you guys grow up, and I haven't got a mortgage any more, and you guys are off my hands, then I'll start to do some stuff for myself. My dad finished paying his mortgage in February of 1978. Would you believe that Dad took sick and went into a coma the March of that year? And he died the first of January 1979. So when his mortgage was finished, ten months later he was dead. And that's had a profound effect on me. Because I've

Above: 21 June 1948: The *Empire Windrush* anchors at Tilbury Docks, Essex. Over half of the 1,027 passengers give Jamaica as their last country of residence.
© Daily Herald Archive/SSPL/Getty Images

Left: *Windrush* passenger 'Big' John Richards (far right) was among those temporarily lodged in the deep-level shelter at Clapham South until they found employment and housing.
© General/Topham Picturepoint/Press Association Images

Right: The *Windrush* brought a variety of skilled workers seeking employment, from mechanics and carpenters to tailors and shoemakers.

© General/Topham Picturepoint/Press Association Images

Above: While many early West Indian migrants mixed with whites on the shop floor, discrimination in Britain was rampant.
© Bert Hardy/Picture Post/Getty Images

Right: In October 1959, Dr David Pitt from Grenada became the first black candidate to stand for Parliament in the UK. © PA/PA Archive/PA Images

Above: From the late 1940s, 40,000 nurses and midwives from across the Commonwealth were recruited to help build the fledgling National Health Service, which was suffering a staffing crisis. © Meager/Fox Photos/Hulton Archive/Getty Images

Above: Workers at the GEC, Swinton, South Yorkshire, 1962. Many West Indians came to Britain with a 'five-year plan' to train or work and then return to the Caribbean. Most, however, stayed on . . . and revolutionised modern Britain.

Below: Religious practice has been at the heart of the Caribbean community in Britain. But upon arrival, West Indians found most 'white' churches operated a colour bar.

Above: Like the church, pubs also became a focal point for the Windrush generation. But similarly, many establishments discriminated against black people. *© Charlie Phillips/Getty Images*

Above: From Oswald Mosley's black shirts to today's English Defence League, successive generations of Caribbeans have had to fight overt, covert and institutionalised racism in Britain.

© *Evening Standard/Getty Images*

Left: Over 50 years on from its inception, the Notting Hill Carnival is still the biggest celebration of Caribbean culture in the UK and an homage to the Windrush generation. © *Frank Barratt/Getty Images*

Above: From 1948 to the early 1970s, many West Indian families were separated for months, even years, as parents working in the UK scrimped, saved and borrowed the money to bring their children over.

© Charles Hewitt/Picture Post/Getty Images

Right: Malcolm Willidon and John Mills outside the Metro Community Centre, Notting Hill, London, in August 1979. The sign behind them says it all.

© Mike Moore/Getty Images

THIS CLUB IS NOW OCCUPIED BY THE YOUTHS UNTIL T I.L.E.A MEETS FOR TALKS WITH U

Above: Up until the early seventies, Caribbean foodstuffs and cuisine were in short supply in Britain. Today, even McDonald's serves a Jamaican jerk chicken burger.

© Romano Cagnoni/Getty Images

Above: 24 May 2011. Mourners gather at the grave of Cherry Groce, whose wrongful shooting by Metropolitan Police officer Douglas Lovelock left her paralysed and sparked the 1985 Brixton riot. Ms Groce had emigrated to Britain from Jamaica as a teenager.

© Charlie Phillips/www.nickyakehurst.com

Merchant Shipping Act, 1906, and Aliens Restriction Acts, 1914 and 1919.

P.M. 22

IN-COMING PASSENGERS

Returns of Passengers brought to the United Kingdom in ships arriving from Places out of Europe, and not within the Mediterranean Sea.

Notes (a)—All Passengers brought by such ships are to be included, whether arriving from European or from non-European ports. 1st Class, 2nd Class, Tourist Class, and 3rd Class Passengers are to be entered in separate groups.

(b)—In the case of those ships which are engaged in pleasure cruises starting and ending in the United Kingdom the full particulars required by this form should only be furnished in respect of those passengers who embark at a port abroad and disembark in the United Kingdom.

Ship's Name	Official Number	Steamship Line	Registered Tonnage	Master's Name	Voyage
M.V. "EMPIRE WINDRUSH"	181561.	THE NEW ZEALAND SHIPPING CO., LTD., 138, LEADENHALL STREET, LONDON, E.C.3.	14414.24.	JOHN G. ALMOND.	From TRINIDAD, KINGSTON, TAMPICO, HAVANA, BERMUDA, To Tilbury

Date of Arrival 21. 6. 1948.

NAMES AND DESCRIPTIONS OF BRITISH PASSENGERS

Above: The original *Empire Windrush* passenger list. Aside from West Indian migrants and British servicemen, passengers from Mexico, Scotland, Gibraltar, Burma and Wales made the transatlantic voyage, along with two stowaways. © *The National Archives, ref. BT26/1237 (1)*

Below: Campaigners on their way to the Home Office to protest at the British government's handling of the Windrush deportation scandal. By August 2018, potential Windrush cases reported to the Home Office had exceeded 5,000.

© *Wiktor Szymanowicz / Barcroft Media/ Getty Images*

been seeking for some answers, you know? If this man, who was as far as I am concerned a good man, who fathered me and my siblings and took care of us, and at 56 – this man always his dream was that when you guys have grown up and are off my hands I'm going to do some things, do some travelling and all this stuff – when he was very unwell my mum convinced him to go back to Jamaica for a holiday, so he went over there in August, '78, and four months later he was a dead man. So that sent me in a deep search. I need some sort of meaning to life. I know I get up, I eat, I drink, and I've got a roof over my head, and these were the things Dad was always drumming into us – you're not a man until you can provide a roof over your head and clothes on your children's backs and food for them to eat. As far as he was concerned, once you've done that you can call yourself a man. That was drummed into me from a wee lad growing up. So I just could not make sense of him bowing out. That's what led that quest. I was saying, 'Look God, if you're up there somewhere I need some answers.' Because if my dad was a good man, and he took care of us, and his dream was to do so-and-so, and he's just bowed out like that, then where do I get hope from? That's what kind of led to me starting to look to myself, look within myself, ask myself some pertinent questions. Am I living in relationship to my fellow man? Am I selfish? Am I so self-centred? And all of these things led me to a place where I thought, you know what, maybe, maybe there is a force out there – call it what you like – 'cause most of us from the Caribbean, we're all believers. We might not be devoted, but we're believers.

With my main job, because manufacturing is very challenging and you don't do the same thing day in and day out, nothing is mundane and routine, so that kept my mind active and kept me in the front line. But I got made redundant, and I decided it was just as well I still have the driving school as a back-up, so I can still feed the family. So I did what I have to do to keep the big wheel turning. And then my ex-manager from the place I got made redundant from got himself a job, and his secretary rang me and said, 'Look, they're looking for engineers at this company, send your CV in.' So I sent my CV in, but I didn't hear anything. Two weeks after that his secretary rang me again and said, 'Did you ever send that CV in? Because we haven't received it.' And I said, 'Yeah, I sent it, and it was addressed to human resources.' Back in those days I think we called it personnel, and she came back to me and said, 'OK, I'll tell Steve.' And then a week after that I got invited for an interview. I went to the interview and did what I had to do.

I came home, and because I had to work and my wife had to work, we had au pairs. So the au pairs would drop the children at school, pick them up, feed them, do the ironing and all of that, up until my youngest son was 12, and then as far as I was concerned he could legally travel on his own. So I did that. I was here one morning – I got a cancellation from a lesson, so I was here – the postman came and dropped some stuff through. I picked it up and I opened it and it said, 'Dear Mr Ellis, I'm pleased to say you've been offered the position of so-and-so', and I sat down and a chill came over me. And I thought to myself, you know what, all this time I thought I was out here doing what I had to do to get the big wheel to turn. And it seems like all along, that power, that force that we refer to as God was in my corner fighting all the time without me being aware of it. Because this job isn't a job I was even considering. I was just doing what I had to do to keep my home and family going, and here I am; I've now got a job back in manufacturing. And at that point I thought what hinders me from bragging and boasting about this guy who's fighting my corner? And it was at that point that I said, you know what – because my wife was a born-again Christian for some time, and I just used the cricket and everything else to preoccupy me – I said to her, you know what, I'm going to come to church with you today. So I went to church and...

Well, the thing is I've always been a family man. Because of my dad's influence upon me, I've always been a family man. I was a rogue when I was young, but by the time I got married the rogue-ism [sic] died a natural death. So my life was centred on the children and making sure provisions were made. So there was nothing I was doing underhand that I'd have to change. I was never a smoker or a drinker, I'd never been a gambler – so because I've always walked the tightrope, the transition was just making that spiritual awareness, you know? But my length of days is not in my hand, you know? That's the point where I said, [God] you win. And I've never looked back.

The only comparator that I actually have is my colleagues who never got the opportunity to travel and those that I meet when I go back to the island. And I see what is required when you're from a working-class background, the jump from working class to middle class – very few make that. Like the salmon going back upriver to spawn, not many make it to the top, do you understand? And I can see where loads of us – I got cousins in Canada, and I got relatives in the USA – all the people that have actually travelled, despite all of the emotions and the traumas that we might have experienced on that journey, they've all lived to a much higher standard than those left in the Caribbean. The elites in the Caribbean are still the elites, but the working class are still the working class. And that jump is very, very difficult when you're in the developing world. So on that basis alone, I feel that the sacrifice my father and mother made to get us here where we were exposed to better education – and most of my family of which I am the eldest have done extremely well educationally, and have done extremely well for themselves financially. And for my children, I've got five children, four graduates – they've all held down very good jobs. My eldest son works for one of the big banks – it's now been bought out by a Japanese bank or something like that, but it used to be Goldman Sachs, and he works there and he earns a fabulous salary. You know, my next son works for LRT as a manager, and he's earning pretty good money. My third son, the one that was very bright and went to grammar school and all that, he works for Chevron, the second largest oil company in the world, and he's here, there and everywhere. Sometimes he's in Kuwait, sometimes he's in Nigeria, sometimes Egypt. He's just come back from Pakistan, so he does all that kind of stuff, and he's done extremely well for himself. My one and only daughter got married in Jamaica last year, and she's done extremely well for herself. So I say to myself, had my parents not brought me here, looking down the barrel, all I can see as a comparator is all the guys I left behind – none of them has really left and stepped up. But because we have the privilege of being brought here, here we are probably when it comes to the status thing – we're not in and amongst all of that, but we're living at a good enough standard, and you can look at your children and think, they're so well-travelled. If they sit back and were to really look and to calculate, they'd think, *'Wow, we're living like movie stars!'* And my children are the very same. They're well travelled. The only continent that they've not yet been – well they won't now unless they go on their own – is down under. Every school trip that they wanted to go on, rugby tour, cricket tour, skiing in California, all of that – now I don't ski, and I have no plan to go on ice, but that's their choice, you know? It would be nice if the society in which we live would give us a little bit more respect, because all of us here that helped to keep the big wheel turning and keep the economy going – we don't seem to get a look-in, only the handful of thugs that go round stabbing and killing each other seem to get all the limelight.

I don't want to make it seem as if it's simplistic, because it isn't. It's a complicated thing. But as an observer, I would put a lot of it down to PG – parental guidance. Until we as a community learn to father and mother our children … but there's a limit to what mothers can do. So as soon as testosterone starts to float around in those boys' bodies, mother can't help them any more. Parental guidance, you know? The guys who grow up on the council estate, they know no boundaries and no borders. If they're out there and they're playing a game of football and it goes over the fence, they'll climb the fence to retrieve their ball. Yet you and I were brought up in a home whereby we've got our fence and our garden, and we'll knock on the door and ask for our ball back. But the guys who come from the council estate, they just pursue the ball over the fence. So it's about mindset, you know? What I'm saying is, the guys who have children and a partner and get a roof over their head – a lot of them have gone back to the Caribbean as millionaires. And the guys who didn't achieve and didn't do a great deal for themselves, they end up in the council estate where you can't choose your neighbour. And that's a massive part of the problem.

I'm not saying that's the complete answer, but I believe that's a big part of the problem, that they've got no structure in their lives. I know a kid in Birmingham. I was up there because I've got lots of friends from school who live there, and I was chatting to this kid and I said, 'What do you do for a living?' and he said, 'Well, I'm a druggie, you know.' So I said, 'What does that mean?' I know what it means, but I wanted him to tell me. So I says, 'What kind of career structure do you see with this?' And I'm saying, 'Look, your days are far better than the days when I was struggling to grow up. Even my day was better than my parents' days. You guys have got it good; all you need is to have an ambition to achieve, and no one will stop you. They can't stop you. If you think your destiny is in the hands of the white man then you're already dead. So you want to think about how you're going to structure your life.' So at that point I said to him, 'Well, have it your own way.' I was trying to show him that there's more than one way to skin a cat, and that you're going down a slippery slope where stabbing or shooting is going to be your portion.

How do you break out? How do you break out? And that's the key, you've gotta break out. Why have none of my children ever ended up behind bars? They had the guidance, right? They had the guidance. And I say to them, 'Look, we're not all goodie-goodies. We're not all the same. But the one thing under my roof which isn't an option, is not doing anything. So share your plan with me. And if you don't know how to go about it, I'll point you in the right direction. I'll know a man who knows a man.'

Well, my dad has influenced me, even from beyond the grave, because he was a very calm kind of person. He wasn't volatile in any way. And he used to say, 'Look Jimmy', and I'd get excited about this thing! And so with my own children, and they've all – bar one – left home, I said, 'You know what, you guys just make sure you have a plan. And where bank of Mum and Dad can get you started, we'll do what we have to do. At the end of the day, I still think that with our generation – although some of these guys have had a raw deal, the guys who had the raw deals are the guys who are the least educated.

ALLYSON WILLIAMS
MBE

Allyson Williams emigrated from Trinidad and Tobago to Britain in 1968 to become a nurse after being recruited by the NHS, which, like many institutions and industries was in desperate need of staff due to the post-WWII labour shortage. But while nursing was to become her vocation emigrating to Britain would fulfil an even bigger personal ambition.

I went to school and I had a wonderful childhood – very social, my parents were very social people. We used to go around in droves – you know, families together – and we celebrated everything. I have wonderful pictures of my parents roasting bacon in the back garden, and that carried on through my childhood. As I remember, I think I was about 15 or 16, before I ever saw television. We never had one. Because these things, you just didn't – you had to take it from America or it cost a fortune in Trinidad. And so everything we did was surrounded by music. We had the radio on 24/7, we bought lots and lots of records all the time. Of course, we had calypso and the steelpan, and my parents were very much into the arts like that as well.

My father played *mas* – that's what we call it, playing *mas* – my father played *mas* all the time. As children we would pack a picnic basket and we had something that we called the Grand Stand or the Bleachers – where there was a stage right across one part of the Savannah in Port of Spain – and all the bands came in and out and performed in the front there, and we judged. And as they came along we would meet their families along the way, and we always had food sorted out for him [Dad] and his friends and so on. So I remember going out and doing that every carnival. And after Daddy and his friends passed, we would go round the back of the Bleachers and play football [laughs], or some sort of game. Because we'd done our bit, we'd seen Daddy and we'd seen his friends. And I remember doing that all of my childhood. And music, we listened to everything. I was one of those that knew every song, every artist that was going at the time. And it was right across the board – it was R&B, soul, country and western, you know. Even some of the opera singers. Edric Connor, who was a singer, he was related to my family friends. All types of music. Anything that was made or was played on the radio, we knew about it.

I listened to everything and I learned the words of songs, 'cause you heard them so often. It was repetitive. Different stations had different themes to their programmes, so it was the same music all of the time. And it came to me, about five years ago when I was here and I belonged to a group here called The Tabernacle Singers – and everyone knew each other – we wanted to do a fundraiser and to go to Ladies' Day at Ascot to help with the tickets and so on. We put on a tribute concert for friends and family and I chose to be Nancy Wilson [laughs]. And it was so incredible to me, because everybody asked, 'Who is that?' They had never heard of Nancy Wilson! So when we were practising and I'd learned the song, they had never heard of it. But I had grown up listening to that sort of music, so it was that deep, that type of music. Because she [Nancy Wilson] was very old school, and it was lovely. When I was 13 my mother took me to see Winifred Atwell in Trinidad; it was my birthday treat. Winifred Atwell was a pianist from South Africa – I was 13 and I loved her and I loved her music. The songs had been on the radio and my mother took me to see her in a huge concert hall – the equivalent of the Albert Hall. And that was one of the things I did quite a lot when I first came to London.

Many people ask me why I look like I do for my age, and I say, 'Because I had a head start!' You know, the Caribbean is the biggest garden to grow up in in the world; you eat everything off the trees!

I think most people in my time were very much into music because it was one of those things – and we always had artists coming to Trinidad anyway. I think it was just how you developed as a family – because I had friends who didn't go, I used to be used as the model and I used to have to beg my friends' parents to go out with me, because I was the most active and most social of my bunch of friends. But as far as I remember, the key thing about growing up was music and the parties and going to the beach. We would go to the beach and every weekend we would choose somewhere different. And you'd listen to music while you were there. So it was just part of how we grew up. We never had television so we never missed it. We didn't know that much about it. You would go by some people's houses and see different television set-ups and stations and what have you, and it was interesting. But it was not something that we craved. Now they have all the different networks and my grandchildren are always vying for more expensive and better phones and all sorts, but we communicated perfectly well. We had landlines, and so that's how we kept in touch with everybody.

We understood it [*mas*] – not necessarily from school but from reading and hearing the adults talk about it – that it was a throwback or a consequence of the slave trade and the abolition of slaves in the Caribbean – in America and then in the Caribbean. It was a form of mocking the white slave masters, because they were the ones that had the costly balls all the time, and the slaves just had a look-in while we would serve these people their food and what have you. Seeing them to their carriages, that kind of thing. That's what we were taught and that's what I read. In the background they would mock some of the masters, but then of course when they were free they decided that they would continue to celebrate. And I know in Trinidad there was a lot of controversy about it because it was banned initially; the governor-general wouldn't allow them to carry on with that tradition. But eventually it worked out. And then also they had to fight to have it follow the religious calendar, because it was how it got accepted that it was a form of celebration. But at the end of that they would repent, and it would be Lent. The outfits, the fashions – you'd put all of that away and you'd go to church and repent your sins etc. So that is how they managed to fit it into the church calendar. And it has moved with the church calendar ever since the end of the 19th century. So the traditions started to evolve.

What I remember is the – what do you call it – the painting, the mud painting and what have you is symbolic of how they used to drum the slaves if they misbehaved. I read that somewhere, that they would drum them in molasses or paint or oil, mimicking the tar and feathering. And then there's the big Dame Lorraine costumes – all of that came from mocking the masters who used to dress like that. It continued to evolve, so the people started to create their own way of celebrating the important themes. And most of the bands in Trinidad that I remember in my time had historical themes. They went back in history and would create costumes to match the period of history.

The bands, each band, should have a theme. Because your costume is supposed to be interpreting something. Otherwise it just doesn't make sense. But the themes have evolved into fun and fantasy, contemporary and historical. As my daughter says, 'The *mas* is the message.' So you have to be able to interpret the theme that you've chosen, and people have to recognise what your theme is supposed to be from the costumes that you've produced.

I think Trinidad in particular – because we also had the calypsos that were a form of commentary and very mocking of the establishment – I think the carnival evolved with the calypsos. Everybody has it, but then Trinidad excelled at it and developed it further and further and further.

I think carnival evolved earlier and faster in Trinidad [than other parts of the Caribbean] because we were bigger and more advanced and more interested in the social commentary. And more interested in developing the carnival to become almost a tourist attraction, although it was never considered like that initially. But then it became something that tourists came to.

It's official that it [Trinidad] is the most cosmopolitan country in the world. Because when I went to school, we had a lot of pure white girls in my school. And they were born and bred in Trinidad; they'd never lived or been anywhere else up until that point. And they were clearly descended from all the sugar plantation owners.

When the slave trade was rampant or in full swing, they used to bring indentured labourers from China, Africa and India. Most of them came from that part of the world. We also got some of the Africans and the Syrians – we had a lot of Syrians in Trinidad who were the business people; they came to Trinidad to trade and ended up staying. But the Indians and the Chinese, what they did generally was they worked on the plantations after slavery was abolished, because they still needed people to work. They joined all the Africans in the farms and the sugar plantations. Because we used to export sugar, molasses and coffee – all sorts of things were grown to a huge extent in Trinidad in the 20th century.

Trinidad sells so much natural gas. Seventy per cent of the natural gas that's used in America comes from Trinidad. This is why it is so soul-destroying that Trinidad is in the state it is. We have the largest deposits of asphalt in the world. And they sell all this stuff all over the world for people to use for the roads. They have so much of – what do you call it, when they make the additional products that come out, umm – by-products of the trade, and they make so much plastic. Trinidad is involved in all of that, and yet there is still so much poverty.

In my opinion, Trinidad was a wonderful place [to grow up in]. It was quiet, but very social. We did a lot of activities, even in school. We had our parents involved in all that we did. We had college football, and it was a huge thing – intercollegiate sports they call it – I played hockey. We did everything in school, like tennis – it was very forward-thinking. I mean, I went to the best school in the Caribbean, which was in Trinidad – Bishop Anstey High School, and that was quite something, to get to go there. We did what we call home entrance tests, and in my year there were 5,000 girls and boys who did common entrance to go to the big secondary schools, and I came 13th. My mother always said that I was a lucky 13. And so I got my first choice, which was Bishop Anstey High School. It was very progressive and very forward-thinking. My headmistress was from England – she was from Reading. And so there was quite a mix of Trinidadian schoolteachers, English people and Spanish people who taught me. My French teacher was born in Paris. It was good because in the French class we couldn't speak English; she did everything in French. It's the only subject I got a distinction in [laughs], because I loved it so much. I thought it was very, very forward-thinking. The teachers really wanted you to progress and be good. We did a lot of concerts whilst I was at school, and plays that were open to the public. And of course we had the sea! We had the beach. So we socialised and one went all over the country on a Saturday or a Sunday.

Well, the time I started thinking about what I was going to do for the rest of my life was when my mother said to me, 'Allyson, you have to remember: life is not one big party. You think life is one big party, but you have to live and think about your future.' As I said, I always celebrated everything. And of course loads of your friends do, too. When I got to 18 – I was 18 in July, and by November, I could drive. So then I got to borrow Mummy's car [laughs]. We went even further afield in this car. So it was that sort of life, and it was lovely. And after A levels I was working at the Ministry of Education. So that was considered a job for life. I mean it was quite a difficult thing, to get into the civil service. My mother was a nurse, so she had a lot of contacts and she knew a lot of people. She had her own social circle from when they were growing up, and then of course they went on to do different things like work in the civil service. My father went to work for the Americans on the naval base in Trinidad in a civilian role. He was fire chief at the time. And so when I left school I didn't really know – you automatically had to go and work, or people thought you would go to the civil service. I mean nursing and midwifery was the furthest thing from my brain. I wanted to do languages. I loved languages. I wanted to speak French and I wanted to be an interpreter at the United Nations in New York. That was in the back of my head. And then I suddenly changed my mind and did biology and chemistry for A levels – I don't know why. Probably because I started to think about that question, 'What are you going to do for the rest of your life?' And, 'Life is not one big party! All you do with your money is party and take photographs!' – and I was a brilliant photographer – 'You take photographs and you give them away as if you're making money [laughs]!' But I think I was between 13 and 16 when I recognised my mum's job as a nurse and midwife.

She used to talk about visiting women, you know, privately. She had private clients. And she would deliver them in their homes. And I used to say, 'That must be nice', and, 'That must be interesting', and it would be in passing conversation. And then one day I said to her, 'Can I come with you the next time?' It just kind of came into my head. And so the next time she had a woman in labour she took me. I think that is when the seeds started to grow. I was about 16; 15 or 16 anyway. She said, 'You just have to sit quietly and look', so I did, and I thought it was the most amazing thing I'd ever seen. I was there for the whole labour. And then we jumped in our car and drove back home. It took us up until about four in the morning; we started out at about evening time. Because that wasn't my mum's job – she had a job running a clinic for the government railways. She would look after minor injuries and she had an assistant who helped. But she was there nine to five. It was very flexible; they would swap shifts to pick us up. I think it was eight to four she worked, so she used to pick us up from school at four.

I was the eldest of five siblings. I had two other sisters and two brothers. The other thing too was that most of my mother's other friends were nurses. Before my mum got this job in the clinic, she was a junior matron in the hospital. There were many, many times when I would walk through the hospital looking for her. My mother's maiden name was James, and her married name was Ley – l-e-y – so she was James-Ley, but everybody called her Jamesy. They'd say, 'Oh, are you looking for Jamesy? Your mum has gone to so-and-so', so I knew the hospital fairly well in Port of Spain. And my mum would take me to little functions and things like that.

And then when I was 16 and doing my O levels – we were living in country – I went to Port of Spain and stayed with my aunt, who is a matron. And she had this absolutely beautiful flat that they gave her out of her job, in the nicest part of the hospital grounds. And they even brought breakfast to her. They had room service for every meal! I stayed there with her quite a bit, too. If she was going over to the ward for something she would ask me to come. So I did have a lot of insight into the nursing profession. I went with Mum that first time, and I went once after that as well. So it sowed the seeds. And so I thought, 'Well, you didn't do French A level, and you have science. Why don't you do nursing?' you know, talking to myself. So I talked to Mother about it and she said, 'Well, you have to go to the Ministry of Health, because you can't just pick yourself up and go to England. You have to be formally accepted by us before you go, because they have this programme on, where they're looking for nurses.' When I spoke to that same aunt I stayed with, I said, 'What do you think about me doing nursing?' And the first thing she said was, 'Don't do it here. Go to England. It's the best place, because if you're qualified in England then you can go anywhere in the world and not do any more exams. So then you are free and you can come back. But train in England.' And of course because I chose to come to England I had to go through the Ministry of Health. I was interviewed by a panel and then they called me back and they finally said that I was selected.

Our nurses never left. They'd leave and come straight back. Because my aunt who I stayed with – soon after I did my O levels – she was sent to London to train, because they were going to develop a CSS Department, which was a Central Sterilising Services Department. To do everything for the procedure you had to be specially trained, and you had to buy the right equipment and buy the right quantity of equipment, because everything was done in a huge, huge department, and she had come over to set it up. So she came to London to train. That's right, I tell a lie – it was before I started secondary school even, at 11, because she was the one that sent me my schoolbag from England. So I would have been 12, yes, because my bag was the talk of the school [laughs]. It must have cost a fortune! But she sent that to me to go to school and I had it throughout all my school years. I remember going to collect it from the post office. It was a surprise! She did say, 'I've sent you something for school, I hope you like it.' But I thought it was a pencil case [laughs]. It was this big satchel; it was so nice and I used it all the time. So she was in London, and she did all the courses and bought everything on behalf of the government. They identified the building and installed everything, and I would go and see her there. She created all the trolleys and the trays for surgery; for hip surgery, brain surgery, she created all the sterile trays. When she came back and set them up she then trained other people how to use them. The interesting thing in the civil service in Trinidad is that when you're in the civil service, you can take your holidays whenever you like. There's nothing about losing anything, nothing has to be carried forward. By the time she did that and came back to London, she said, 'Oh, I am tired now.' She trained several people how to run and set up the department. She said, 'I need a holiday.' And when she went to check, she actually had a year's annual leave of holiday. And I said,

'What, 52 weeks?' and she said, 'Yes!' She hadn't had a holiday for about ten years because of this big project she was involved in. She had to see it through till the end. Her training was about a year in London. So she took it all. She took it all and went around the world.

England was foremost in our minds and in our heads and in our hearts. Because it was the mother country. Everything we did – our exams were marked with Cambridge or Oxford certificates; about 30 per cent of our teachers were white middle-class English women; everything we learned about, all the kings and queens – all that was English-based – English literature, everything. Everything was about the mother country – the Commonwealth, everything. So it was all there in our heads all the time. My thoughts were that I would go and explore and see what it was all about, and then come straight back home. Most of my office colleagues thought I had lost my mind. I was working for the Ministry of Education. I worked there for two and a half years. I was promoted twice. And then I announced that I was going to England to study nursing. They thought I'd lost my mind, because if you're in the civil service it's a job for life. Nobody leaves the civil service. That's one of the things my mother used to say, 'I agree that the civil service is a job for life, but you're not going to go far unless somebody drops dead!' But I was lucky that I got promoted twice. They would say that I would do well because I worked well. If I had chosen otherwise or didn't know what I wanted to do, I could have stayed in the civil service – I'd probably be prime minister now! Or a parliamentary secretary or something. A few of my friends who worked with me have got top jobs in foreign affairs. But it was a purposeful choice, because I could have stayed where I was and done very well. It was a deliberate choice to study and get into the nursing profession – but to do it in England, because I was advised that there was the best place to do it.

My mother always said that you always want your children to do better than you. She always said it. All of that was in my head, and I thought, 'Oh, then I'll be the first', because none of my family had left yet. They hadn't gone anywhere. I thought I would be the pioneer and go to England and do the nursing training that was considered to be better than in Trinidad. But I thought that I would come back and continue to do well. That was the idea.

I think that you could actually do anything you wanted to do [as a woman]. Nursing and midwifery was considered quite a good profession. But there were also people older than me who did want to go – I mean, I said I was the pioneer within my own family, but other families elsewhere had people who went to do medicine, say for instance at Harvard University or in Jamaica. Two of my school friends also went off just after me to Scotland to do medicine. All parents said the same thing to their children: 'We want you to do better than we did.' A lot of my friends who went abroad, their parents had never left Trinidad. My parents had never left Trinidad at that point. So it was always that notion that your children would move on and eventually move out.

I was actually terrified! I was only 21. I was much more terrified about it than my mother was. We had this conversation and she talked about missing me but said that there was a phone and she'd always be in touch. She was a very strong character, very particular about the way you talked, about the way you dressed, and about how you addressed people. She would always make us call her friends Auntie or Uncle, or Mr and Mrs. She said that they were her friends and not our friends, so we had to have some respect [laughs]. When I was ready to leave, because I passed the interview, they called me back to offer me dates as to when there were vacancies, and that's why I had to wait. I had to wait about a year to go, and that was when I was 21. I said to Mother one day, 'You're so excited about me going to England, but you won't be able to watch me the way you watch me here. Everything I do, you're on my case. So, what do you think will happen when you're not there? I can do anything I want.' And she said, 'No you won't', and I said, 'How do you know that?' She said, 'Because you know the difference between right and wrong, and because you were well brought up, so you won't do anything you want. You will do the right thing.' But you know she was absolutely right – because I could have got into all kinds of – but now! My friends thought I was a snob – I always had my head stuck in the air. But it was because I would object to certain things, doing certain things – because I would always remember my mum saying that I knew better and that I knew the difference. And she was right.

When they call you back and offer you a place – there are several hospitals that have intakes – they will tell you the dates of the intakes and the position of where these offers are. There were positions all over England, all over London and the South East, Birmingham, the North, Scotland, everywhere. And I deliberately chose to stay in London, because London was where everything was and there was a lot to see and do. It was easy to get to and from the hospital, and there was all the sightseeing. All the things you learned about in your history – from the Tower of London to the MCC – all of that was in London. So that was my choice: London. I asked them, did they know about all the hospitals they chose – they showed me St. George's, King's College and the Whittington in Archway. And they said that the Whittington was a favourite because there were lots of West Indians up there. And I said, 'Well, that's it. That's the one.' Because you felt that you had some kind of kindred spirit there. And that was how I chose it. So then they had the next intake – and I got in in May 1967.

It was probably about nine months between getting in and coming to England. And that was when I chose the Whittington. So you choose and then you inform them and then they start writing to you. They start writing to tell you about the hospital or about London. They speak about the hospital, where it is located, and what the training entailed. So I knew by the time it came up that I was going to the Whittington and I knew where it was. I had all the letters of introduction, and so on. By that time I had to get a new passport, because I'd had a British one but we had become independent in 1962. And so they confiscated all the British passports and I had to get a Trinidadian passport. They had to get my passport to the Ministry of Health because they had to take it to the high commission to get the student entry visas. All that was done at that time. The interesting thing with me was that during that time – around the same time that I was being selected to come to England to begin nursing – it was announced that the Trinidad government had asked the Americans to hand back the airbase, which was on the north-east of the island, the nicest part of the island, with the best beaches. Well they [the Americans] had a 999-year lease, and that's where they were stationed – but Trinidad wanted it back. So they started talking and negotiating about when it would happen, and so on. And then of course they started talking about the work – the Trinidadians who worked for them and the American school for Trinidad, and all this sort of banter was going on. Just when I was selected to come to London, they [the Americans] announced that they would give permanent residence to all the Trinidadians who worked for them, if they wanted to come and live in America, and for their families and their partners and children under 21. And I said, 'Oh, just as well I'm going to England then', because I was excluded anyway [laughs].

America never appealed to me, before then and since. Although at one point I did think of it – but we'll come back to that story later on. But yes, I was excluded from it anyway because I was coming up to 21, and it was supposed to be 21 and under by the time all the negotiations happened. And I think it took another couple of years to work out, even after I'd come to London. So that was what happened in terms of me coming here, because the rest of my family did go eventually to America.

Well, I didn't know anybody that was already here, funnily enough. But of course we got the stories, like with Lord Kitchener, his name and the pictures on the boat – we heard all those stories back at home. But it didn't relate to you, so it didn't really matter. It was just part of what was happening at the time. So it didn't really impact in a negative way or a positive way; it just happened. I mean I knew that I was coming to be a nurse at the Whittington and that it was a place with lots of West Indians. So I had a sense that I would meet like-minded people and we would be able to socialise like I knew it, cook and eat the same way. It was only when you actually came here that you realised you couldn't find all the stuff!

Well, two nights before I left I had a farewell party! They said I'd be too tired, so two nights before I had a farewell party with all my friends and people from the office, everybody. They brought me gifts and it was lovely. It was really nice! Everybody was excited for me, and I was excited. But it was interesting because I was more excited about flying as I was going on a Pan Am jet. But what had happened between my selection and my actual going was that… well, the family would be getting a permanent residence in America, his [Dad's] application was being processed, and so on. But they still hadn't decided if they wanted to go, because it was a huge uproot for all the family. My youngest sister at the time was eight. By the time I was ready to leave, my dad had gone to America two weeks before. And so I said, 'Oh, good opportunity! Can I go to America and stay with you and see you?' So that's what I did, I went to New York for a week. And then I flew from New York to Heathrow [laughs]. And that weekend we went to the Empire State Building and the Statue of Liberty; I did all the tourist things in New York – the United Nations, too. I used to have a pen pal during my teenage years, and he had gone to work in the United Nations building after doing his master's. So I met him and he took me around the United Nations. He was a Bajan and he'd gone to do his master's in America and then had got a job. So I did my tourist bit and then visited aunts and uncles, and my godmother lived in America. Then I came to London after that week and a day, something like that.

All the friends my dad introduced me to when I went to see him – my godmother and so on – they all seemed very affluent. They were very well off. They were very settled and were doing lots of interesting jobs, a lot of them in the healthcare profession. They just seemed to be quite together and well off. And so I thought, well this is what happens to people who come here – you actually do quite well. And that was my first impression. I mean I have never got very deeply involved in the politics of it, but it was just how they presented themselves. They did seem to work very hard. That was the original impression I got. As opposed to when I got to England and I thought, you know, what is happening here? This is supposed to be *the* mother country. I was shocked when I came to London. I was very shocked. I suppose it was the remnants of the war, but a lot of it was so dull and so dark. I didn't know at the time that that was how British cities were built, with all these houses joined on to each other. It was just quite depressing, really quite depressing – and difficult to conceptualise. Even though you know that it was ravished by war, you still expected – I mean you did see Buckingham Palace standing grand and tall – but you would just go to work in hope of understanding what was happening.

I didn't think I'd made a mistake. I did think it was going to be a horrendous experience. I mean, I cried for about three months solidly because it was so dark and grey. Despite arriving in May, it was cold, and we made such a fuss of the cold. And they actually put everything out of sync – because in the hospitals they turn off the heating in May and put it back on in October, so they didn't care what happened in between – but we made such a fuss that they put it back on for the rest of May [laughs]. Because we complained so much! I used to cry. When I got to the Whittington I found out my set was 32 girls all starting at the same time. Eighteen of us were from the Caribbean, and about six or eight of us were from Trinidad, and none of us knew each other. And everybody was surprised that none of us knew each other. They all thought it [Trinidad] was this tiny little dot. So I didn't think I had made a mistake. I just thought, *This is not the mother country – what happened to this place?'*

It was three years for nursing and one year for midwifery, probably another year for experience. It was the five-year plan, and then I was going straight back to Trinidad.

My landing was incredible. The flight was great. It was wonderful. I never had experienced it. I thought it was really good and we landed here safely. I got to Heathrow and I thought somebody would pick me up. I thought that I would see somebody. I stood around and there was nothing. Nobody. So I looked around and I looked around. And then this man came up to me and said, 'I have noticed you have been here for the last hour. Is there something wrong?' And I looked at him and he was a nice-looking guy. I said, 'Who are you?' and he said, 'My name is Fitzroy, I'm Jamaican. But I've noticed that there isn't anybody here picking you up.' And so I told him that I thought I was being picked up by the authorities because I was going to the Whittington Hospital to start my nurse training this week. And he said, 'Oh my goodness, I know Whittington very well. One of my best friends is nursing there. If no one comes to pick you up by the time my girlfriend comes back, if no one has picked you up by then, I will take you.' So the girlfriend came and he took us both to London. And he said, 'Oh you must be hungry', because now it's mid-afternoon. So we stopped at a restaurant and had dinner. And then he brought me up to the Whittington and he took me to the place where his friend was – there were no phones, I mean you could phone but they frowned on you – and he said, 'I'm just hoping and praying she's at home, in her room', and he went and found her. And she came, and I mean she's one of my closest friends on the earth. And she said, 'Oh, you're supposed to go to the office', so she took me to the office. And they all were having heart attacks – because when I got here, I didn't look at the papers properly and it had told me I was supposed to get on a coach to Victoria. So they had been up and down three times between the time the coach would have come in and then. They thought they'd lost me [laughs]. That was my start to life at the Whittington.

If my mum had known I'd got into a car with a random guy and his girlfriend, she would've said, 'Are you mad?' But I always had, I mean – you thought of that as a kind person helping you. We didn't have that kind of fear in those days, so I never thought of it as anyone wanting to do me any harm. We didn't have things like big burglaries where I grew up.

Well now I know where he went, because we went to somewhere in Ealing to eat. So he did go up the North Circular and then down the A1 into town.

At first, I thought London was a bit shabby. Everybody looks so dark and everything looks so dark and there's lots of smoke coming out of chimneys. And I thought, *'God, what is this place?'* It was really dismal. And then, of course, as I said, with the crying and thinking I wanted to go home, I rang my mother to tell her eventually, and she said, 'Well you didn't go to London to like it. You went to study nursing and midwifery. So just get a hold of yourself and get on with it and stop being so babyish.' She said you didn't go to like the place. That's what I kept saying, 'I don't like this place, it's so dark, it's so depressing, so dismal.' So once you truly understand that you have no choice and that you have to stick it out, you change your perspective. You begin to understand why it looks like it does, or you begin to bother to think about why it is like that. And you made an effort; you made an effort to make friends and you made an effort to go out.

I got close to some of the girls and we would go and explore the Underground. We didn't know how to read the signs or anything, so we would just jump on a train, and on the inside we'd see which stop would come next and if we thought, *'Oh, that's not the way we want to go'*, we'd jump off! And we'd find out which train was going in the opposite direction, and that's how we started! That's how we got around. We would visit anybody who had family. We would team up and ask, 'Can I come with you?' If anyone had a family or an aunt – I had a friend in my class whose aunt worked at the high commission, so I used to say, 'Can I come with you?' And I would go to the high commission in Hyde Park Corner quite a lot. And I got to meet different people – when we would come, her aunt would occasionally take us shopping, so we would go and explore High Street Kensington or Harrods with the aunt who had been working there for a long time. So you teamed up with people, and I mean … in the 40 years I've been here – is it 40? Nearly 50 – I've been to Madame Tussauds about 20 times! And the interesting thing is that you become the icon in London. Everybody that wants to come to London after that point wants to come to you. I have had so many people stay in my room sharing a single bed because they're in London. You know, I have friends who are air hostesses and they come and stay with me. And so you have to find out everything about London – you have to find out all the prices, where there is to stay … And then of course what happened to me was that by the end of 1970, or at the beginning of '71, my parents decided to go to America. So they did uproot everybody and they went to New York. So then I ended up going to New York like two or three times in that year. And so my focus became New York rather than Trinidad. I carried on doing my tourist bits and meeting people. Every time I go, I go to something different; I'll go to Madison Square Gardens, or I'll go to Broadway, and do something a bit different. So it was interesting, because then that became the focus and that's when I realised that I didn't really want to live in New York. As soon as my parents got there, they loved it, and they started talking about me joining them there once I'd finished training. And I had just made up my mind – just after my mother flew over in 1974 – I said, 'OK, OK, I will come and give it a go.' My mother said that even though I'd trained in England and it was the best, they still had their rules. And you had to do what is called a state board exam, and you had to do that before you got your registration as a nurse in New York. But any other state you go to has its own exams. They do them slightly differently. I had just decided that I would come. So she found out all about what it would entail, and I realised that I hadn't done psychiatry in all of my training. I chose to do neurosurgery instead of psychiatry, as something different. The state board exams were in five parts: medicine; surgery; obstetrics and gynaecology; paediatrics; and psychiatry. So I had only done four of the five parts, and I had to do a psychiatric course. We decided that I would go and do the first four parts and then come back and do the psychiatric course, and then go back for good. But in the November before I went to do the four parts I met my husband – this is November 1974.

We probably had a lot of house parties. A lot of house parties, and that was good. I mean, mostly West Indians – so we had the calypso and it was close to home, so that we really enjoyed. We would look after each other. I used to be very happy because I got to drive everybody around. I could drive and I was not a drinker; I didn't like alcohol particularly. So our friends would go to the parties and make sure I understood where we were going so I could drive them – I was the designated driver for a long time! And I loved nothing better, because I loved to drive. I really enjoy driving. So that is how we did it. We would fill up cars. The guys would come to the nurses' room and we'd pile in, and I would sit in the front because I'd have to look and see where we were going. They didn't always get drunk, but they got quite tipsy. But of course by the time I'd dropped them all back, they'd sobered up a bit so it wasn't so bad [laughs]. We did a lot of that. We went all over London: Croydon, Maidenhead, North London, Central London. And another thing we used to do a lot of was go to concerts, you know, go and see artists. I have seen a lot of people in concert.

The first big concert I went to see was the Jackson 5. I've seen the Fatback Band, Anita Baker, Aretha, Bob Marley and the Wailers. You know, the one person I regret that I didn't see, and that's because I went into labour, was Marvin Gaye. But I still got four times as much as I paid for the tickets! And quite soon after that, he died. Who else did I see? Patti LaBelle, Ashford and Simpson, Al Green, Isaac Hayes. Who's that other one? Barry White – I used to go to all of them. I went to see Hammer, M C Hammer. I need to think about it, because I haven't been anywhere for a while. Who did I see the last time? The Temptations; Lionel Richie was also one.

We did have things to do at the time, a lot of concerts and parties. But it was a combination of all of that – something to do, something that you'd never forget going to down the line. I mean, when I moved house the other day I had 108 programmes from cinemas and theatres and concerts I'd been to.

West Indians like to keep hold of things, but it can turn into hoarding. I don't understand why that happens, but it is very, very prevalent in the West Indian community. I mean, I have some friends [who hoard] and I can't bear to be in their home for long, because I feel as if all their stuff is closing in on me, you know?

I have seven Trinidadian passports that I keep. This is the difficulty as well, because when we ask people why they hoard stuff they can get very offended. I asked my friend, 'Why? Why do you have all this stuff?' And she said, 'Well, because I could always use it. I don't always know if I have it, but when I'm old and I have no memory I'll still have it from back home.' So, I said, 'When you find out that you have it, why don't you stop buying?' Because what I find about hoarders is that they're very wasteful; my friend is very wasteful. She buys things that she sees and that she likes and they will just stay there. She will open a packet of something and then it'll just stay there. They're very wasteful. And she throws away so much food. But they can't see it.

I think I started to hoard, especially foodstuff. Because I'd see it on sale and think, *'I'll get two more.'* One day, I remember going into my cupboard and thinking, *'What is all of this? What is this stuff?'* I'm taking it all out and putting it back bit by bit and I'll collect some for the church. I had to literally open and throw away 21 tins of stuff that were out of date by two years. And I thought, *'Now, that is disgusting and sacrilegious.'* I went to a friend's in – somewhere down the end, in Kent – or Hampton? Or Clacton-on-Sea or something – but my friend came from Trinidad to look after her mother and went to visit her in hospital. She said that she was going to go and tidy up. She said, 'I don't know how my mother lives like that.' We started in the kitchen and I'd never seen anything like it. There were hundreds and hundreds of tins of stuff out of date by four years or five years. The mother made such a racket when she came home the next day.

My daughter, she tells me I'm a hoarder. She says that she doesn't know anybody who has 42 pairs of shoes [laughs]. I don't know what it is for me with clothes and shoes, it's just liking something and then you will have it. You don't know when you're going to wear it and you don't need it to go anywhere, but you like it and you must have it. And the thing is, you put it away and you have that notion all the time. So eventually when you're putting away the third or fourth thing you bought, you see the first one again and think, *'Why do I do this?'* But you never stop. It comes from gratification, to prove that you can.

House parties were such a significant part of socialising for people from the Caribbean at that time because everybody was familiar, it was small, and it was in someone's home. So it was family-oriented. We used to call them bottle parties. Anybody would bring a bottle and that was what everyone did. Some people would be designated to do the food and the rest of the people would bring a bottle. And so that way you got around the cost of having it in a hall. You would have weddings and big things like christenings in halls that you might rent, but most things like birthday parties you would have in somebody's home.

Also it was a place you were guaranteed to get food, because somebody's going to cook up a pot of rice and peas, or a curry. So it was really a West Indian social gathering, the house parties and bottle parties.

Yes, there was always food. The West Indian notion of, 'Are you going to come over on Sunday or Saturday evening?' That was food. Our social life centres around food. Even when we moved and I had people coming to help me, most of it was on Saturday and Sunday. I had all of my husband's friends coming on the Sunday, so I cooked rice and peas, macaroni, cannelloni and chicken, and he said, 'You did all this in this empty house?' And I said, 'Well, yes!' That is how we live. You reward people or you thank people or you invite people to your home, and you share food. You sit down like a family and you share food with other people. It's also because you like your traditional dishes and they're nice to share with people. But it's always been about food, always. You are expected, as one West Indian to another – if I invite you over on a Sunday or a Saturday, as long as it's evening time, everybody knows that they get something to eat. If they tell you, 'Well, I can't stay long', then you'll do something quick [laughs]. You know, like you'll do a rice and pea salad. If they were staying longer for a proper dinner you'd have starters and dessert even.

The first thing I ate when I came here in 1960? I can't remember what we ate – fish and chips or something. But the food in the dining rooms, I had never seen anything like it. I had never seen so much potato in my life. To be honest, I had never seen the type of vegetables that they cooked; of course in the Caribbean our vegetables are yams, sweet potato, plantain, eddoes, dasheen. Um, what do you call it? Grapefruit, I had never seen. I'd never seen broccoli – broccoli, and so much carrots and cabbage. I had never seen potatoes like that, because the only time we ate potatoes was in a potato salad, cut very fine with diced carrots and peas. Or they were in the curries in Trinidad. So I'd never seen boiled potatoes or roast potatoes or anything like that. It was just quite shocking, and tasteless – utterly flavourless. But then of course it was another way that we socialised. We met in the dining room, and from May to October they took the money out for our meals. So there was breakfast from 6:00am till 8:00am in the morning; there was coffee from 10:00am till 11:00am; there was lunch from 12:00pm till 2:00pm; there was tea from 3:00pm till 4:00pm; and then there was supper from 6:00pm till 8:00pm. And then from 8:00pm till half-past there was supper again for night staff. So from May to October we all met in the dining room for each of these meals. Whether you're working or you're off, you came to the meals. So as a result I went from nine stone to 14. My best friend went from about seven stone to 11. We all put on masses and masses of weight, because we wanted to meet, and we met at mealtimes. The 18 of us in one class would meet at mealtimes. And then we suddenly felt, *'Oh my God! Look at what's happened to us!'* It was incredible, because we were just eating the food they presented.

In those days you had to live in the nurses' home for three years. You had to be there; you weren't allowed a flat. Because you were being trained, they wanted to make sure you were there and everything was accessible to you. Most of the nurses were foreigners as well, so they wanted to make sure that you were safe and well throughout your training. They were quite good, really.

They used to come out of the woodwork [men]! They were everywhere, because one of the girls would have a cousin, who had a cousin, who had his best friends from the office. And another one would have a brother that she never met, and he would have his friends. It was just like a whirlwind of men; they were there all the time, always. They were very generous guys; they would take you out and take you all over – the Hilton for dinner, all sorts of things. Very charming. But the interesting thing was that a lot of them were African, and only a few were West Indians. I was proposed to like nobody's business. But I said all along that I would never marry anybody but a Trinidadian. And I used to tell them, 'I'm sorry, but I have already come 5,000 miles to London. I'm not going even further afield.' But because I was so in love with Trinidad and Tobago – my culture, and the way we work, everything we had to offer, and the way we socialised – that I wanted my children, if I ever had any, to be close to where their parents are from.

I met people four years ago when I went to Trinidad – I met this woman who had just come to Trinidad for the first time in 32 years – and she was so flabbergasted by what I knew and the fact my daughter was there with me. She said, 'How do you do that?' And I said, 'What do you mean?' She said, 'You know, if you have any interest in your country, I don't understand how people can stay away from that.' But I suppose there are different reasons why people come away, and why they never want to go back.

I mean a prime example of what made me feel like 1,000 million dollars: one year – well the kids always went home with us, and only last week my son brought up some steel band music from Panorama,* hearing my daughter playing – but we came back, and as I said friends are always around my house, and my daughter [Simone] had a couple of friends over for the weekend. And I heard them talking in the room, and she was telling them about Panorama and carnival and what have you, and one of her friends said, 'I don't understand, you have to explain this to me. I don't understand where you're from – because you live here, but you know so much about Trinidad. Exactly where are you from?' And Simone said, 'Well, that's no problem. I am a Trinidadian. I am from Trinidad. I just happen to be born in London.' Well, I thought that was the greatest thing I'd ever heard, because it just made me feel like I'd fulfilled my dreams of giving them something to hang on to that they understand.

It was when I met my husband, Vernon, that he started telling me about being a founding member of the Notting Hill Carnival.

* The UK National Panorama Competition is a steel band contest held annually on the Saturday before the Notting Hill Carnival at Emslie Horniman's Pleasance Park, London.

Well, going back, I had decided that I would go to America and give it a chance. I was going to do the four parts to the exam and come back. I'd booked myself on the psychiatric course from March to September, and then I would work and go back in December and stay. And in November 1974 I met a friend who said she was cooking for two friends who had come from Germany to go to a party, and that I should come and join them. I'd just come off duty, so I said that I'd have a couple of hours' sleep and then I'd come. So I went, and we ate, and I had to cook and it was lovely. And then they said they would like to take us to this party. It was a guy called Johnnie who was celebrating a big birthday, and I realised that I knew who it was – in Hampstead.

We were in Finsbury Park, so it was still fairly local. So they ended up going to look for booze, but of course in those days booze was so hard to find. They ended up in Leicester Square, and they came back very late, and I said I didn't feel like going. They begged and begged, and Shirley begged and begged, as she didn't want to go as the only girl. So we ended up at this party at 1:00am in the morning. It was in full swing, and we chatted in the house – it was a nice house with three floors. I was dancing by myself and Shirley left the room. But I decided I would look for them after about half an hour. So I saw her talking to these two men, and waved to her and went across. She said, 'Oh, don't worry, I'm here. You look worried.' And I said, 'Well, I just wondered what happened to you and if you were all right?'

When I saw these two guys – my husband, my future husband – I hadn't seen him or the other guy before, but I thought, *'Oh my God'* – he was just commanding, standing there. So she said, 'Allyson, come and meet Dan.' This guy, I think he was Dan Jackson. 'This is Dan, he's an actor.' And so I shook his hand. I noticed she didn't introduce me to the other guy, but I didn't say anything. We started chatting and I asked him what he had done, so he told me the things he was in. This other guy is still not saying anything. Eventually I got the courage and I said, 'Oh, excuse me, what did you say your name was?' And he said, 'Well, actually, I didn't.' I was so staggered! I said, 'Fine, cool, I'm so sorry.' So I sort of turned and started chatting with Trin, my friend, and then I said, 'You all right?' And he said, 'Fine.' So I said, 'I'm going to go back to my friends to dance. Dan, lovely to have met you', and I went back into the room. I thought, *'I'm not going to say any more.'* But as I got to the door I felt a tap on my shoulder: 'Excuse me', and it was him! And he said, 'May I have this dance?' And I said, 'Oh, you do speak!' So we went and we danced and the first thing he said was, 'I'm so terribly sorry to be so rude. My name is Vernon.' So I said, 'Oh, you have a name as well. Pleased to meet you.' And that was it; he never left my side for the rest of the night.

By about nine o'clock in the morning, I said, 'Oh my God, I am so tired. I really have to go home. Let me find my Shirley and the guys and see what they're doing.' So I found her in the kitchen, and she was making bacon salt fish [laughs]. She said, 'Oh, I'm just going to fry this bit; why don't you stay up for breakfast?' And then we were thinking about going, but I said, 'God, I don't think I can hold up', and he said, 'Don't worry, I can take you home if you really want to go.' And I said, 'Oh, can you? Thank you very much.' And there again, I don't know this guy from Adam and he's taking me home! But it's Hampstead to Finsbury Park, so it's not that far. So we went and he stopped outside my house, and he said, 'I don't know about you, but I am really starving. We should really have stayed for breakfast.' I said, 'That's a point, now you talk about it.' And he said, 'Don't worry, let's go for breakfast.' And he took me to … the Cumberland Hotel I think it was, for breakfast [laughs]. And I thought, *'I have never been taken to breakfast in my life!'*

Then he took me back home, and he said, 'Oh, by the way, I don't have your number. I'd like to call you', so I said, in quite a cheeky little sense, 'Well, don't call me. I'll call you.' And so I gave him a bit of his own medicine [laughs]. This was, of course, Sunday morning now, and when I got inside, my flatmate was doing her nut – she wanted to know where I'd come from, whether I'd been out all night – so I told her and gave her the story, and she said, 'My God, that sounds serious!' And I didn't call him until Wednesday, Wednesday night. And you know, on the first ring he picked up! But it was a dilemma for me, because I was thinking, is he really that nice? But I was totally not bowled over by him. I said that I wasn't going to be pushy. I had some hours off, but I did other things. And I thought that I'd ring him on Wednesday night, so if he doesn't want to see me I can just go to work! He said, 'Oh my God, I have been waiting all this time for you to ring. What are you doing?' I said, 'I'm getting ready to go to work', and he said, 'Don't go until I see you.' And he came straight to my flat and took me to work. The next morning he was there at 8:00am to bring me home. Yes, he did that all the time until I went to New York in December. Anywhere I went, he would drop me and pick me up.

And so the crunch is now: he was going to Trinidad in February for a month, I was going to New York on 20 September and would come back at the end of February. And so I went and my mother was beside herself – she was so excited, because I finally decided I would do the exams and I'd spend some time in New York. We used to argue because I said that I couldn't stand New York and that I preferred Boston, or that I preferred Connecticut. And she said, 'Well, what's the point? You might as well stay in England if you're going to be so far from us.' So I said all right, all right, I'd do New York. I got there and she'd emptied a room and emptied a wardrobe, a big chest of drawers. And she's chatting away and chatting away about what we will do. Suddenly she looks at me and she says, 'Ally, what's his name?' I said, 'What do you mean?' She said, 'I am your mother, you know. And I have spent four years trying to persuade you to come to New York. You finally agreed, and now you're behaving as if you didn't agree to come to New York. There must be some man confusing your head.' And I said, 'Well, yes', and she said, 'I knew it! Who is he?' And I said, 'Well, his name is Vernon.' And she said, 'Vernon?' And I said, 'Oh, I am just besotted by him, I am so in love with him.' And she said, 'But I ring you every week and you have never mentioned this man! How long have you known him?' And I said, 'Three weeks' [laughs]. She said, 'What! Are you crazy? You're going to change your plans of a lifetime for a man you've known three weeks?' I said, 'Mum, I just know. I just know that I will be with him forever.' She said, 'What, are you psychic or something?' Trying to put me off! But I said, 'I can't do it, I just can't', so she said, 'You're not coming to New York after all?' I said, 'No.' I said I'd do the psychiatric course, because

I'd got a place and I'd go back and do it. I said, 'But I'm not going to do the state board now. And actually I have to go back after Christmas because then he'll be home!' She said, 'Wow. Well you have it bad. You have it bad.'

And that's what I did; I came back in the middle of January to be with him for February. And when he was leaving and I went back to his flat, he had cleared it and put stuff in storage. He'd cleared out one side of the wardrobe for me and said, 'This is your side.' And I said, 'My side to do what?' He said, 'For your things. You're coming to live with me, aren't you?' And I said, 'Am I?' He said, 'Yes you are, but you take your time. Whenever you feel like it.' So he'd left me the flat with his car and his keys. By the time he came back, I had moved in [laughs]! And the rest is history.

The nice thing – he always used to tease me about my bottom – and one day, my daughter said to him, 'Daddy, tell us how you met Mum.' And he had us all in stitches, the way he described it from his perspective. It was incredible. He said that when he saw me coming towards him, he froze. He had never seen anybody so beautiful in his life. He said, 'When your mother asked me a question, I don't even know what she said. When I opened my mouth I was so rude. And she turned her back, she didn't even tell me goodbye. She turned on her heels, and this bottom! I'd never seen somebody with such a tiny waist' – because of course I was getting to 14 stone and I was thinking, *I'm not having this.*' So we all went running. And I used to dance in Trinidad, so I did all the exercise I could to keep fit. And I had this tiny little waist, and he said, 'And when she went into the other room, her bottom was still coming out.' It was so funny.

I had no idea that I would meet anybody. It's not that you went and there were several guys lined up – you went to a party with a friend. And I never believed in love at first sight. Never, it was a load of rubbish. I mean you find somebody attractive, and you might chat with them, and it works out that they go their way and you go yours. But I think that it was truly love at first sight. When I first saw him I was absolutely bowled over. And when he was so rude I thought, *'Oh, here you go, I just got it wrong.'*

But that is the thing, even though I said that I was sort of besotted with him, I didn't know he was a Trinidadian. I suspected he was – it's Trinidadian men who are arrogant! The pose, you know? I didn't know, I just suspected. I didn't know from the accent. I couldn't tell. But I knew, I knew somehow he had to be a Trinidadian. And I was right [laughs]. I thought, you know ... with the arrogant pose and the chest up [laughs].

I never noticed any mixed couples in the Caribbean when I was growing up. It probably was there and it probably happened. I always thought of them all as Trinidadians; I never saw the colour. There were some guys who were half Chinese, and there were half white girls – but they always talked like Trinidadians, so you looked at them as a Trinidadian. I had Chinese friends. My best friend was a white girl from school and we kept in touch for a while – she went to Canada and I went to England. And she had the same birthday as me. And so it was easy for us more than anywhere else to associate with mixed people, because we grew up with them. Was I surprised about Meghan and Harry? Yes, yes I do think so. I think it is probably the best thing that's happened to the Royal Family. Even though they had Queen Charlotte before Meghan. She [Meghan] is well brought up and cultured and well spoken, so I think that she will bring the best of the blackness in her to the Royal Family. I think it's a great thing.

I think in a way it was inevitable that, even without the Windrush, there would always be a lot of people coming back and forth to England. The Windrush is just highlighting what was inevitable, because a lot of people would have done it anyway. But of course it's not been given a name like that. Because they were invited – it was like an assumption that it was a generation of black people that were invited here to help Britain. So I think that it was inevitable.

I didn't have many white friends, but my uncle was married to a white woman, so my cousins were all mixed race. But I was in awe of the ignorance of the normal English citizen, who had no idea of the rest of the Commonwealth and said the most outlandish things. They were very racist and said things like, 'Don't touch me, your blackness will rub off', and 'Where is Trinidad?' and 'Where are all your tree houses?' And of course when you took pictures to show them – I used to take my albums – and they saw my mother's car and the big garden and the big house. I said, you know, 'Look! Are all the houses stuck together? We do have cars and roads.' As I said, my secondary schooling was all about the English – English literature, geography, everything was about the English. So you assume that the English are as well educated as you are. It was a shock when I realised. Because I knew where every country in the world was by the time I did O levels, and you assume that everybody else knew – so why are they asking me about what part of Jamaica is Trinidad, or what part of Africa? And where is it? I just assumed they were as educated as we were.

They were doing their thing. Everybody just goes their separate ways. And in my circles, they were never as accommodating as your fellow black workers. No, I would get invitations from my uncle to family dinners and so on, but not to anyone else. I suppose to their minds we all stuck together and would go around with each other as West Indians. But they never came forward, as such, in those early days to say that they wanted to be included or wanted to include us. Occasionally, some colleagues would invite you to the pub with them. But of course, not being interested in drinking, it's not my favourite place. And I had English friends – well I do now – who would have birthday parties in the pub. It was very different to the concept of a West Indian party. So it never really took off. I must admit, we did get the odd invite – but to a pub, not to somebody's home.

NORMAN MULLINGS
MBE

Norman Mullings has been a pillar of the west London community for sixty years. He has performed a variety of public service and community-based roles, from being a school governor to sitting as a magistrate, and is widely respected for his equality and civil rights activism.

When I came here in 1958, no sooner had we come here than we faced the Teddy boys. And while we were facing the Teddy boys, you have police brutality on the other hand, and a lot of the police believed that *we* were the ones ... although we were the victims ... we were the ones who upset the Teddy boys. So, they [the Teddy boys] have a right to kick hell out of us. And instead of protecting us, police were brutalising us. And so that was the 1958/59 period. We had to start looking at how we could help one another, how we could start doing things, and that was when I became very involved in establishing an organisation called the International Friendship Council, to look at how we can come at racism and how we can stand up for ourselves.

Although one may feel that we have [anti-racism] legislation so people are more inclined now to behave themselves, now it's more subtle. Racism is still as endemic as it was in those days. Only now it's more subtle, and it's being used in a different way. We don't have the blatant racism, we don't have the Rachman and we don't have the signs 'no blacks, no Irish, no dogs', but you go for a job and it depends upon your name and your postcode – you ain't gonna get a look-in. So, you know, it has not gone away.

To a lot of people who want to be accepted, they forget these things and they feel like it's people like me who's a troublemaker, cos I'm always raking up old coals and talking about slavery and calling people racists, when, if I behave myself, who knows? I may even get called to the House of Lords, and all that! 'You'll never get a CBE unless you're nice to people,' they say, but I say I will always have to be who I am. Now if the CBE comes I may go for it or take it, but if it doesn't, it's not a big thing. I remember when I was awarded an MBE in 1993. I had a number of people giving me grief and saying I should 'send it back'. They say, 'How can you take something, you know, that is part of the slave mentality?' But when someone refuses it, they normally make a big song and dance out of it. It's not going to change the system.

I remember when I was appointed a magistrate 30 years ago, I had the same argument. How can a black person be a magistrate and then send people down or refuse people bail? Well, quite often, everything starts in the magistrates' court; not everything is indictable. For a lot of young people, their first bite of anything is at the magistrates' level, and even when the case is heard, it's when you go into the retiring room, that's where the decision is made, not based on the evidence, when in fact it should be based on the evidence. In the retiring room it's gut reaction. People feel if you're shifty or you didn't look me in the eye, you must be as guilty as hell! And why would the nice policeman come along and tell lies about you? He has no axe to grind! I have always said to them, the doubters, let's look at the evidence, and of course a lot of people feel that if you keep hounding the police they start to dislike you, as if it's going to worry me! That's my life.

I believe in fair play and I believe in justice for all, not justice for some. Just because you have wealth and power you don't have a different kind of justice towards you from somebody who hasn't got it – you know that's just not right. And I will never ever accept that thought and logic. But a lot of people feel that in order to get on, sometimes you must turn a blind eye. How often are you going to turn a blind eye? A lot of people may feel, 'Well, it's all right for you 'cause you're going nowhere, but I want to get there and I have my mortgage and I want to get on. You're just old and miserable!' But I have always been like this, even when I was young.

It comes from my grandmother. I'm influenced a lot by my grandmother. I was brought up in Jamaica in a family where, yes, I had my mum and my dad, but my father's mother lived with us, and she was the matriarch. She determined what we did. My sisters and my brothers and other people who passed through that household have her to thank for a lot of things that came to be.

There were seven of us siblings. Some of them are alive now – we still have five. Two have passed away. And all of us have managed to do quite well. All of us have my grandmother to thank. And the good thing about it is she never pushed you – she would just sit you down and come out with some gems. She would make sure you understood what it is to live a decent life. Being a decent human being does not mean you're going to let people walk over you; but don't walk over others either.

She was a very firm black woman. A Jamaican woman who, because of her Christian background, you know it was one of those things that you must go to church – that's not negotiable! You are going to church – you can stop going when you are old enough to say, 'I'm not going any more!' Then, you can stand up to her. But until then, you *will* go to church, you *will* come in at a certain time. You will also not expect your sisters to wash dishes and think *you* can't wash dishes because you are a boy! Because, when you have a wife and she's sick, how is she going to eat? So, these are the sorts of basic things to start off with. Just because you're bigger than somebody, don't bully them. And don't let somebody bully you either. But look and learn how to stop somebody bullying you, or how do you try and stop them bullying others.

Jamaican machismo? Yes, of course … we don't like anyone to know we are going to the kitchen! So, whilst we are at home and we carry out our duties, when we come out we deny that we go near the kitchen, because 'that's a women's place'! You know, before you know it you'll be talking about hanging out clothes and taking clothes off the line … but we know where the power lies, and a lot of black men, the majority of the black men in certain areas, if it was not for the woman holding the purse strings they wouldn't have a roof over their heads! So therefore, if it's such a macho thing, how is it the woman that holds the purse strings?

Now a lot of men also got hurt in the process because when they start to get too macho and they have to leave, they find that quite often their name wasn't even on some of the title deeds. You know, they trust the woman so much that they have been misled. That has happened as well. But when it comes to the majority of black men, you usually have the woman who rules the roost, she deals with the kids. The only time he comes in or he has any part in it is when she warns them, 'Wait till your father come home!' because that is when she finish her bit and that's his additional bit. If you don't behave yourself, when your father comes home, he'll deal with you. But that's the only other thing – she is the one who determines what will happen.

The majority of mothers, especially in Jamaica, the mother plays a fighter's role in the way you've been brought up. Yes, fathers have their say and fathers take decisions, but usually, it's women. And my grandmother in our family, she was the woman who was always there, and she was not going to put up with any nonsense! She would challenge my dad, she would challenge my mum, she would challenge all of us. She was a woman that we all looked up to. She gave us that stability. She inspired us. Her motto was, 'Do all the good you can, to all the people you can, in all the ways you can, as long as you can.'

My grandmother used to come out with some gems. For example, we are from a rural part of Jamaica where we had animals, and she used to say that if there is nothing wrong with you, you must get up and help to take the goats out, and the pigs out of the sun, and water them, if nothing is wrong with you. And during the day, if we have one sweet potato, we must share it amongst *all of us*. And before you go to your bed at night you must thank the Almighty for what you have done that day. You can't go wrong with those basics. People may think, 'My God, she's a philosopher', but she's a basic, basic woman. A strong black woman. Stubborn as well! She ain't gonna stand no nonsense. You have to convince her. I remember going back to Jamaica after I came here, and I go back and spend a couple of nights with her, and she would say, 'Look, I'm going to lock the door at eight, so if you're not in, you're not coming in.' Yes, it's her rule. It's her house. And she would say, 'When you start to pay the rent then you can turn in when you want, but not till then.' And she's not going to compromise.

The majority of the people in that part of central Jamaica mostly had strict upbringings. Yes, you also have the exception. You'll have those that are spoiled, you'll have those where the father feels that the boys shouldn't be in the kitchen, and so he spoils them. Or you may have children from a single-parent family who may have a different outlook on life. I suppose it takes all kinds. But the family I'm from… we had a strict upbringing, and it has not done us any harm.

We were from a working-class family. My father was a cabinetmaker and a carpenter, so he was the one who was earning all the money. My mother very rarely went to work, although we had a canning factory not far from where I was born, and she used to work there during the crop times; sometimes she would, sometimes she wouldn't, but we are from a background where Dad earns the money. My grandmother, when it comes to farming, she did a lot of things, but a lot of that was because she had a lot of land, and so she was able to have people who farmed some of it, and of course when they farmed it they had to give her some of the crops, and you have to pay her for the land. And she was very shrewd in terms of how she managed her livestock. She always had so many goats and so many pigs and so many sheep. She was a woman who was always selling things and making a lot of money. So, we were a working-class family, but we weren't too badly off, and we were not hungry.

My grandmother, and my father and mother, now that's where they come in, they are the ones that impose the discipline, and they, like most Christian people, don't believe you should spoil the child. They are not going to beat you for everything, but there must be some level, where you must respect certain rules. For example, if you're told that you're not going to the cinema till the weekend, cos the cinema was some distance from us. You had two theatres, you had one Odeon and the other one I think was an ABC if I remember, and you were told, if you did everything like they told you to do, you carried out all your chores, you made sure you chopped the wood for the cooker, you moved the goat out the sun, you watered the pigs, you do everything, and then come weekend and you want to go to the cinema, you may have done something, so you're not going. You are not going, and so you would normally wait until when they retire and you'd climb through the window, because you're going! Now of course you have to bribe your brother because you're sharing with your brother, and it depends on how much you do; your brother may either grass on you or he may decide, well I will have to, you know; it's like blackmail in a way. Each time you get your dinner you take out a bit of food, to give to him as payment. You can't say nothing. It looks like you're being kind, but he's reminding you about it. And you know there may be times when I get a chastising for breaking the rules by going off to the cinema, or when you're coming back and climbing through the window ... and there's your father, sitting down at the bottom of it!

Well, you know it's your brother that grass you up. And you're going to get a hiding, cos he told you not to go. Now I'm not saying it happened once or twice, it happened more than once or twice. And I had a friend whose father had a car. And he used to borrow his father's car without his father's knowledge. And off we all go. Boys will be boys. Notwithstanding how disciplined you are, that is that kind of background. You know and you know it's part of life. Part of growing up. So, when we have young people doing certain things, I'm not condoning it, but I'm using my own experience.

They were very hands on. My parents were that, you know, they were the ones who loved their children, and when I talk about loving their children, not because they love them, they spoil them. Because they love you, well, they want better for you than what they had. And for that to happen, you will have to follow close to the path. And you could not stand up and argue with your parents. It's only when you get big and you can say to your mum, you can't slap me any more, cos I'm big now. And sometimes, you know, we're not all sociologists and psychologists, and sometimes words, the words don't come, so if the words don't come you have to grab them and sometimes shake them a little. I'm not saying it's the ideal thing, because quite often, regardless of how sophisticated you are, your kids drive you to a point where you want to go crazy! Where do I go from here? I would shake you but the law says you mustn't, and the society I'm from, they're not going to shake you, they sit you down, and nobody interferes. There is too much interference in how you bring up your children nowadays. And sometimes that is not for the best intentions. And also when you are running, you know, maybe skipping a bit, but coming from that kind of a background you can imagine what it's like for some of those parents as well and some of those of my age range who came through that, and then you were here and told you can't talk to your kids too loud, cos you know, that's abuse, and you're only talking, you haven't touched him yet, and you must not do things that were considered Victorian or Draconian, you're too harsh.

When you go to visit your grandparents, you ask permission to take things out of the fridge, so why do you want to walk over your mum and just pass her and take it out of her fridge. You see, so if you look at it this way, that because we are from Jamaica, Guyana, Trinidad, we have to follow this, sort of, all of our textbooks are printed in Cambridge, when we go to school we have to speak the Queen's English, we may cut off into patois and different dialects, but there are things that you don't cross, cos that's what your parents want you to be. You are going to come out to be something, and even if they have to beat it into you or beat it out of you. There are some bad habits they will beat out of you. But the habits that they want, they will have to instil those into you. No, it means that in order to stay within that, you sometimes have to be devil's advocate. You may want to do something, and you question your parents why you can't do it.

And the other thing I was fortunate with was that my parents were prepared to talk about anything I wanted to, and they were open, and because I was in a home where we all eat together, it was one of the wonderful things that over a meal we'd talk about most things. And although my father was always never there for mealtimes, but when it comes to weekends, especially Sunday after church, we would all eat together, and when we eat together whatever you'd been doing throughout the week would be a part of this discussion. And that to me, even now, I look forward to a meal on Sunday when I have my grandchildren around and my own children and the family, because there is something about it. People who eat together and pray together, stay together. Yes, but there are times when you have to have differences of opinion, and it's good, and it's not that you resent your parents, it's resenting what they represent. They represent authority. It's not the parents you resent, it's the things they tell you that you can't do. And the other thing is, we are from a background where age matters. Like we say uncle, or sir, or mister, or ma'am to people that are older than us, and you can't call a big person by their first name, and that's what your kids and your age range tends to do. You feel it's all right to call a big man by his first name. No, that is not heard of where I come from. And so, you know, it's not that we have kowtowed or we are timid, but it's because of our mannerisms.

We had a lot of people who say, 'I'm no African – I'm Jamaican!' And you try and say to them that all of us are from an African background, but if you feel like you're a Jamaican, so be it, if that makes you feel good. But remember that we are all from an African background.

Back to eating together, though, they sometimes had shift work. And you know you may only have one weekend off in three, and there are so many things happening that weekend that you may not have the time to sit down. So one can understand that, but even if it's not every Sunday you should try every now and then to sit down over a meal. If you can do that, all the things that you have boiling... you know it's like a kettle, there is so much steam in it, and you have to get it out, especially when you have a heap of children around, and how they've been getting on at school, what's been happening, have they been having some problem with the neighbours, having a problem with somebody else, or you may have gone and spent time with your uncle and you come back, tell us how you relate to your cousins when you were there. These are things that have got to be fed in.

I enjoyed my school so much. When I came here, I'd gone through my secondary education, and went on to do my Cambridge Certificate. So I did those and I did two terms at Clarendon College before I came here. And so I came here and I had to start the A levels all over again, and I went first to North Western Polytechnic. That was in Kentish Town, but now it's in Gospel Oak. North Western Polytechnic became part of Middlesex University, but that is where I did my A levels. I remember when I went there, the admissions guy was saying that you're fortunate you've done English at Cambridge level. And I was wondering what's so surprising about that – I'm from Jamaica where English is the spoken language. 'Oh well, I can't understand some Jamaicans,' he said. 'That may be so,' I said, 'but you may not understand somebody from Liverpool, somebody from Manchester, somebody from Glasgow, because you know you have variations in language. They are all speaking English, but if somebody from Liverpool was trying to communicate with you, you don't believe it's English?'

All through schooling, one of the things that really made me was I had some really good teachers, and I remember them. They were exceptional, notwithstanding the limitation in resources; those teachers were competent. The same teacher who did English could do maths, the same one who did maths could do geography, the one who does geography could also carry out biology and experiments. So this is where you have teachers who were proper teachers. You did not have to move from one class with your rucksack into another. When you go into that classroom, you're gonna be there until you go home.

And even when you went to secondary school, the same thing. Yes, for PE and things like that you had specialist teachers. I was no good at games, but I'm chairman down here of the Learie Constantine West Indian Association. When it comes to cricket, whether they can play the game or not, there is a passion. I will normally go to Lords with them. But I normally go for the frivolities, the beer and the fun, and I am fortunate that most of the people in a lot of the West Indies are cricket fanatics. And most of them belong to the Middlesex County Cricket Club. So when you go there, even if there's a lot going on, I can go. If I have the time I will go for the beer and that sort of thing. But I am no good at games. I am no fan of cricket, I can live without it, but of course when the West Indies are here, we can get a coach and we go to Edgbaston. We go to Nottingham, wherever they are, we all go and buy a cap. To go and come back to say you've been. But I am no good at it. And the other thing is I love music, but I am not a great fan of reggae, so a lot of people call me a philistine, cos I like to listen to soul stuff. How can you? You are from Jamaica, you must love reggae. I don't, really.

The other thing is, I am a participant. I will do all the things that they want me to do. So, I will go to the cricket matches even though I don't understand the game; I will go for them. As I say, I go for the frivolity, just as I would go with my friends from lodge; it's part of the camaraderie. Same thing with football. My grandsons are avid Arsenal fans. So when Arsenal are playing, and before Arsène Wenger was replaced, they were always going to buy another player, they were going to appoint another manager, and they know the team, and I used to say to them yet I have to take my grandson still to the Arsenal shop, so I have to share my pension with them. So when football is on, I can live without it but I still watch the game, although I prefer to go to the theatre, and I say you know not all of us like the same thing. And of course the other thing is it depends upon what's happening at the cinema and a lot of my friends give me stick for that as well, you know, that I'm not from that traditional Jamaican background. 'You love cricket, you love reggae and you must go to the horses; what's wrong with you?' I've never been able to. I don't understand how to put on a bet and I'm not going to try. We're all seen as gamblers.

If you're black, you've got to be Jamaican. You know we have less than a million Jamaicans living in England, but tell that to the media out there, because every time you see a black man he's got to be a Jamaican. You even have the media who say he looks Jamaican. What does a Jamaican look like? The media, the police say it all the time. He sounds Jamaican, he looks Jamaican and therefore he's got to be from Jamaica. Most of the kids out there chasing people with guns and knives have never been to the Caribbean. They were born in Hackney, in Lambeth, in Brixton, in Harrow. They have never been outside of the United Kingdom. But we are seen as these black kids from the Caribbean. No, they have to be Caribbean, because we have pigeonholes in the way we portray each other. If you are from Nigeria then you are a fraudster, that's your role. If you're from Ghana you are going to do everything that is evil because, not just fraud but any kind of documents you want you will find it from them. All the Caribbean islanders are seen to be Jamaicans, so as a Jamaican you are the man who is going to shoot somebody or you're gonna stab somebody or you're going to sell them drugs because that is what we are good for. And what is so sad is that you have people who are enlightened who fall for that whole argument, and I remember talking to an eminent person who still believed that Jamaica was part of Africa! Yes, and this is someone who has been to a couple of our public schools. But that happens.

Eventually, I learned to take their ignorance for granted. Don't forget, in the Caribbean we had missionaries. They were nice Christian people who were sent out there to turn us into good Christians. Because the Church of England were always sending out these missionaries or evangelists and they were going to evangelise all of us, we are going to learn our Bible better. A lot of my Rasta friends say to me that the white man take away your gold and gave you the Bible. And you still have the Bible and he still has the gold. But when they sent those nice people, they did not expect that one day some of us would end up here. Because they came out, we treated them with utter respect. We were very kind and generous. We would do fundraising to buy them a car. We had no car, we had to walk or get public transport, but we did not want the missionary to walk in the hot sun between churches, so we would all buy a car, we'd all save up and we'd all buy a car, at harvest we would sell everything we had grown, so that we could get a car for the good missionary. We call him parson. Parson in the Caribbean is the missionary that come out.

So, we do not want the parson to walk around in the sun, so we get him a car, and we may have to get someone to drive it for him, and that is how we treated them until we arrive here. And realise that some of us want to go to church as well and were told you can't come in; we don't want to see you too often because they didn't expect us to be here. As a matter of fact, the British government, when they were drafting legislation looking at the Commonwealth, they thought that because we were so far away, the Commonwealth to them is Australia, Canada and India. You know the likes of us in Jamaica ain't gonna come here, because the fear would be too much to bear and the journey is so far, not realising that sooner or later the aircraft would come down to the point where you can get cheap flights. This is that whole thing about how do you keep them out? So, because the aircraft are now carrying them in, we have to pass legislation to keep them out. Because we never realised that they would come in. If you listen to the argument today around Heathrow being crowded, the manager from Heathrow is saying people from Australia are nice people, they shouldn't have to wait at border control – let them in, and they are our friends. They are not saying that about the Caribbean people. You have to keep an eye on them because they could be carrying drugs, but the ones from Australia, New Zealand, Canada – let those nice people in. Absolutely don't keep them waiting, don't let them stay in the queue like you and I, because they are nice people. But your grandfather or your uncle who's never been here, those people that fought in the war and went back and are coming in – you must give them hell, grill them. That's how we see things, so in a way when you came here, yes at first it was a surprise to me that these people should be much more enlightened, but then you realise that when you have working-class communities, they don't travel very far, and the majority of working-class Britons have never travelled around the world. They used to go to the Isle of Wight and Guernsey and places like that, and it's only in more recent times when we have the Freddie Lakers and others that came on and they start to do charter flights; they start with just one to Spain. They never had a passport before, so they didn't have to travel. But you know, talking about passports. If you want to take up citizenship of this country, you must know all about Britain, but ask the man down the pub what he knows about Britain, and he was born here, and yet they want me to tell them all about Britain, and I was born in Jamaica. So, we are talking about fairness here.

It was just a thing that a lot of my friends were travelling. I think it was a chap called Earl, my close friend, who was going off to Canada, cos you know we've got people who have gone to Canada, and don't forget from the early days people were going to America for farm work. But we have people who were travelling off to America, and we had a relative who had come here before, and don't forget long before 1948, people were coming here, and some of them who were in the RAF didn't go back. So, I wanted to come and my uncle was living in Brixton, my uncle Alton, and I said to my parents that I'd love to go to England, and they said, 'Right, there is a chance for you to go there and you can then do your studies, go for five years and you can come back and be a teacher.'

I was going to be here for five years. I came in 1958. When I came here I was just passed my 18th. I was coming up to my 19th birthday.

Honestly, I wasn't too clear on what the economic situation in Jamaica was at the time. We had a little money, but as far as I'm concerned, we weren't short of much. And those days, of course, we were still using pounds, shillings and pence, because it was not yet the decimal days, and my parents could find the fare for me. So you know it was not a case that we were too badly off. So they had to find £85 to buy the plane ticket to get to England, although £85 was a substantial amount, but they could find that. And I remember my grandmother selling her goats and things and giving me the money.

I'd flown from Jamaica from when they had the first CARICOM conference. It was in Trinidad, and, as a schoolboy, I was in part of what was called the 4-H Club, the agricultural programme, and I was very good in terms of cattle judging, because Jamaica has a lot to offer in terms of agriculture, and we have a big show called Denbigh, and I won one of the prizes and that was part of it. So I can't remember clearly about it, but I remember going from Palisadoes airport in Kingston, now Norman Manley airport, and I was away for nearly a week. So, I had been travelling before but this was a different thing, getting on this big iron bird – it was BOAC. So, I'd never gone on one where you had to climb up so far. When you go up on top of the stairs and look down, the earth seems to be a different place, and you haven't even taken off yet.

My mum and my dad were seeing me off. My gran didn't come because she was crying. My mum and dad, one of my uncles and a whole lot of people, and I remember my little case being packed with my few bits of clothes and a couple of ties, and I remember my uncle tied it for me, so you can put it around your neck because you can't remember how to tie it, and I was packed ready to come. But my God, that flight was something else, and then it took off, the first time, and you feel that you go that high, and not only that, as I said this was a flight that took … I want to say 11, maybe 12 hours. It was a direct flight, and it came to Heathrow. This was in September time, so it was fairly mild. When it was coming down, I thought, *'My God, these are all the chimneys.'* I thought they were all bakeries. Yes, because you see the only time we had these steams coming out of the chimneys in Jamaica would be in the bakeries, because we have a lot of ovens for bread and all that, and I was accustomed to that.

I had a jacket on, of course, but it was only because I was fortunate to have a proper jacket and tie, and you had to make yourself look good. And my uncle was there with his wife, and I think someone from his church. So it took me a while, you know, and I can't remember what they asked me, but they stamped my passport, and so I came. Because in those days you had a British passport, but it was granted by the Governor-General, so you were a British subject. I remember them stamping it with some stamp in the back that you have a right to live here, and I come through with my little case, and I'd never seen such a large carousel waiting for my little case to come off. And I also had one of those raffia bags that had bits and pieces in it, and I come through and they were there waiting for me. And then you come out to the big city.

Wow, and those days, of course, you didn't have mobile phones, so you had to call back home to tell them you're here. So my uncle had to send a telegram back to say I've arrived. Yeah, you had to send telegrams but it took around two days or so, and that was it. There was a van, I remember from there to Brixton, You know, funnily enough, I can't remember (the drive from Heathrow). There wasn't the motorway then if I remember rightly because we have the M4 now. We came through Hayes and it seemed like an eternity, but we got to Brixton, and I never forget my uncle. We came down Brixton Hill – instead of coming up we came down because the prison was on the left-hand side – and I remember him pointing that out, that's a prison over there for bad people, and he said anyone who's bad, that's where they go. There are some young people today that think it's a badge of honour. Prison or anything to do with the police, those sorts of things should be frowned on.

You know it's a different world. I remember when we came to his house and his wife. Somebody was cooking before we go there, so there was a meal and we had something to eat, and I was introduced to all his girls. He had about four or five daughters, and then sooner or later he sort of bring me into what I have to help him to do, go to the laundry and take clothes to the laundry, and I thought, *'Hold on, when I was in Jamaica I never had to do things like that.'*

But there you go, anything for a quiet life.

NORMAN MITCHELL

At 98 years of age, Norman Mitchell is one of the oldest surviving members of the Windrush generation. Eschewing retirement, he still runs the centre he set up for the local West Indian community nearly 40 years ago, and travels regularly to his native Jamaica. His joie de vivre even landed him a starring role in the ITV documentary, "Secrets of Growing Old". But what exactly is the secret of his longevity?

It was spotless. It was a lovely service. But I just don't want to see them doing these services. What I want to see them doing is bring back the people. That's the important part of it. The people that dem deport, they want to bring them back. Not the one and two. Because when I went down [to Jamaica] the year before last, there was a planeload coming with 40, including the lady that married the Englishman and the Englishman died, and Mrs May [the British prime minister] said you didn't have no papers, so I still have to send you. And she send her down – 70 years old. There's another lady who went down, to bury her brother, and she was down there nine years. They wouldn't let her come back. She came back eventually.

It was a big ting down there [the 40 deportees].

In 1970, '71, '72, '73, '74, '75 – right up to '80 – Manley was writing in the papers and saying whether you are from Jamaica or any country and you are in Britain, make sure you take up your citizenship. It was in the papers all through those years.

When I used to go to meetings in those days, I would say to those that are West Indian, 'Did you see what is in the paper?' You know what they would turn to me and ask me? Mr Mitchell, what do you want me to do, change my nationality? Hehehe! What you have to do? Leave them to it! Still, Mrs May had no right to do what she done. And she shouldn't be there now, as a prime minister! She should be out! It's wrong, it's wrong.

You know what Mrs Thatcher does?

Up to yesterday I saw the young woman's sister and I said please inform your sister that she is to go to Kingston and get on the government. She has a baby here and Mrs Thatcher wouldn't let her register the baby.

We had a discussion once that babies born in the air, in a plane, is a citizen of whatever country they were flying over. The child is to be registered in that country. So, this young lady was here and she got her baby here. I can tell you where the baby is born, so that's where it should be registered.

Anyway, since the Windrush ting comes up and it's going on, I advised her, for the baby's sake. He's about 15 now. Try and see if they can sort it out and register him.

We're not only speaking about the Windrush. We're speaking about the Windrush family. So they give you up to 1975.

We're all British – our grandparents come from here! Hehehe! My great-grandfather was from here, Mr Lee. He's an Englishman! So when they're going to trace, if they go back to slavery, a lot of Englishmen, Scotsmen, Welshmen, Irishmen, was in Jamaica… And they all leave a mark there!

Mary Seacole … her father was from Scotland.

My earliest memory is from when I was four years old. I was at home with my mother. She was preparing lunch for those that had gone to school. While we were there, about 11:30, the rain, the lightning and the thunder … moving, flashing … and then there was an almighty bang! And when we looked [outside], fire was 'pon the ground. Afterwards, she says to me, 'Come with me, I smell fire.' So we left the kitchen. In those days, the kitchen was away from the house. We left the kitchen and went to the house and she looked all around and she saw nothing. She went back in the kitchen and she say, 'I smell fire, come', and went out in the yard, big yard, and she look everywhere … and she don't see this fire. We went back in the kitchen and she started to cook. 'I smell fire. Come.' Hehehe! We went back in the house. She don't know where this fire is, but there was a fire! We went back in the house, came back to the kitchen and then she look so, around the coffee, she look up in the cupboard. Bam! Fire stand up in the coconut tree! Hehehe! Blazing like mad. She say, 'Come with me.' Her father was still alive, so he wasn't living far. So we walk up to the father's home … old man. He's getting old. So, she told him what happened and he said, 'All right, come with me', and he begins to go down. But at the same time, all the schoolchildren come back … no nothing, no dinner, no lunch never prepare yet! [Laughs.] I don't know what they did eat! [Laughs.]

Anyway, we all went down with the old man and then he send them down in the coffee [field] and tell them they must sweep away all the trash and the leaves from around the coconut tree, so they don't catch alight. The follow morning, all the coconut branches was bowed and the coconut started to drop. The best bearing tree in the yard. Anyway, my father had three people that came in to pail ginger. They came from a place called Alston. When he came and saw the coconut, he say, 'Nothing wrong wid de coconut dem, the coconut dem is all right!' And he start to chop! Nothing was wrong with them, anyway. Because of the fire, they fell off de tree, so. But they didn't waste. Hehehe!

The lightning, the thunderbolt drop on de coconut tree. I'll never forget that. I was just four years old.

I was telling someone the other day, I didn't wear trousers until I was going to school when I was six years old. Not in those days. Just a long shirt. We didn't know underpants. We didn't know trousers. We didn't have shoes, neither. Just a long shirt.

Oh my God. Those days… This was back in '21, '22. Oh yes, we have fun. Play. Those days they call hair grass like women hair. And the girls dem used to come from out the district and comb the grass and plait hair. Yeah, it's true, it's true! So we used to hide – play cheffy. You run and hide. Hide and seek. It used to be good fun, good fun.

Then you had these big flowerbeds with these beautiful flowers, June flowers – it don't bloom until June month. We have the pink and the white, and when you hear dem bloom. Oh my God – there's nothing pretty so. And when you hear somebody going to get married, especially the June flowers, that's the one they used to make the bridal flowers. Beautiful.

I grew up in Middlesex. When I came here, and they then ask me where I'm from, I tell 'em Middlesex! [Laughs.] I came back and live in Middlesex. So, it was a bit surprising to them – they didn't understand. Manchester and St Katherine's and St Anne's are all in Middlesex. Inland.

My father was a farmer, a big farming man. Big agricultural man. Yes, he does well.

Oh, bless me. It was 11 children. I'm the only one left. I was the last one, too. I was the baby. And I'm the only one left. I had a brother that died in 1930. He was 24. One sister died about 1945. Also, my father died in 1935. Then I had another sister died when she was 70; that was 1970. Then I have another sister died when she was 85 and that was 1985, I think. Then I have another brother died when he was 78. He died after that sister. And then one brother died, 2002. He was 92. And my last sister that died … 2013. She was 95. We're all good stock!

What's the secret of my longevity? Hard work! [Laughs.] Hard work. Yes. That's all. I can't put it for nothing else. Because the Lord helped me to return to almost every one of dem funerals. And see that they buried. And that's it.

Now the lands are still there. But the grandchildren, they're no good! We had a property – 11 and a half acres. Was in coffee, cocoa, breadfruits – you name it. Everything was there! Last year when I went down, I went there … hehehehe … I couldn't even find it! Hehe! Nothing but woodland. And I'm very grim. It pains my heart. I can't stop talking about it.

When I ask the grandson why he treat the property like that, he say the last time he pick and chop cocoa, he got 11 and a half boxes. And you sit down and let it grow up in woodland? He went to Kingston go sit down. Without any reason? It's true.

There's another property with six and a half acres. Same ting. One of my nephews, my sister's chile. He give it out to his friend dem to plant. It's true. To plant yam and diss and the other. But I'm going down, Sunday coming. Oh yeah. I'm going down! I have a young lady that went to the tax office and she just phone me, for I pay de tax last year for it. And I phone her and tell her to find out. I didn't know I didn't pay it last year. I paid it the year before. So she phoned me yesterday and told me it is £70. I don't tell her I'm coming. I don't know when I'm coming. So, when I go down there I'll sort that out. I'll give her the money to go and pay. I don't want them to see me, for if they see me they gon' put it up! [Laughs.] No, it's true! If they know I'm there, they'll put it up!

I going to do some surveying over these lands – I don't know if God's going to give me the strength – but I decide when I go down there to buy a water boat. [Laughs.] Oh yeah. I feel God giving me the strength, you know? It's not a far walk to go in the one with the 11 acres, so I get a taxi to take me to the nearest point and then maybe about three-quarter mile you have to walk to go into the field, and have a check-up.

Who am I going with? On my own – I don't travel with people! I don't want nobody to tell me, 'I'm not going there!' or 'I'm not doing that!'

I'm not sure if mango crop run out in July. You have star apple, but you can't travel with those – they're too delicate. East Indian mangoes are going out now. I don't think any fruits ... guinep is off now, too. Plum is off. I'm not going with an intention of getting any fruits. Maybe when I go down I'll get a few coconuts. And relax myself. Hehehe.

I went down last year. But last year I was sick. I went down four weeks, and three weeks I was in the house and never come out. My feet dem just pains. I didn't go to the doctor – I say I didn't want to see the doctor to tell me, 'How can you travel?'

The last week I had down there, I got up the Monday morning, and said, you know what happens? Here's what – I'm going to Frankfield this morning. And I got up the Monday morning and I dress and I call a taxi and I went to Frankfield and I never sit down again! [Laughs.] I was up and around everywhere. I went to Ocho Rios two days before my time expired. I got the coach from there to the airport. And that's it.

When I go down now I stop at my sister's ... the last sister who died. She and her husband died, so the house is locked up. Very nice. In Clarendon. So when I go there now I'm the only one in the house. One night I was there it was like she come and tell me, 'It's time for you to go to your bed!' [Laughs.] No, it's true! I can ... see her. One night I sit down there, the light went. I ALONE sit down in de dark! There's a lamp there, but I didn't know where the matches were to light the lamps. So, I sat there. Anyway, there's a little young man that keeps the house, so it didn't take too long after he came and jus' as he came now I was going to light the lamps, den … de light come back.

I came to Britain in January 1955. Before I came I'd only travelled in Jamaica. I came by boat, the *Fairsea*. I was already married with three children when I came. Two boys and one girl. Hehehe.

Well, in those days, everything was low. Money was low. I left home when I was 27 and then I went on the mission field – preaching – and I spent seven years out on the mission field. I spent five years in St James, Montego Bay, and two years in St Elizabeth. And then from there I left and came here.

When I was growing up we wanted to do a lot of things but we couldn't do it. [Laughs.] I tried carpentry, but I didn't get far with that. I did farming, I did well with that, on the family farm. You know when you reach a certain age there is a motive to … expand. Move out. And then, when I decided to leave home, I had pigs, I had goats, I had a cow, I had a field… Just the other day I was telling somebody, I didn't know I was rich! [Laughs.] No, it's true. I didn't know that I was so rich. But looking back now … I give the pigs, 11 pigs and the sow to one of my auntie-in-laws. I left the cow at home for my brothers. The goats I leave dem in the field. Then the cane, yam, potatoes … I leave everything wit' dem. And I just went. I was going to build a house. I had 1,000 feet of cedar board and plank under my mother's house, in the cellar. I leave everything there. I go back I don't see nothing!

I was a preacher. At first I was doing superintendent work for the Sunday school. Young people's meeting. Then I started to do pastoral work, then evangelist work. Then a district pastor's work. I had a group at church that I supervised. But churches were poor in those days. It was not like today. They couldn't manage. The people dem was poor.

I remember in about 1927 or 1928, men was only working for two and sixpence a week. Government and everything. They call it half a crown. It was somewhere in about 1931, 1932, when Manley, he was a union man, and he called a strike throughout the island. And he told them that anywhere the strike begins and if they are on the line and they are going anywhere they must stop the train same place! Oh yes. So all the trains, like the one from Montego Bay going to Kingston, it was stopped by one of these strikes – on the line, not a station, on the line! The one from Port Anthony it was stopped somewhere in St Mary, the one from Frankfield was stopped maybe going to Chapelton.

So at that time, this man, Mr Fox, was the transport minister here [in Britain] and him overseeing Jamaica. So Mr Fox says this and Mr Fox says that, so Manley let Mr Fox know that there is a strike on and the train dem stop by the way – so they raised the money to one shilling … a day. So, you could get five shillings now for de week. This is true. And that's how the island begins to build up. It was governed by dem here. And that's the way they used to handle us. Then the banana … if the banana shoots 18 hands they call it a 'bunch'; and the bunch they give you two and six or two and ninepence. They call the eight hand, 'three-quarter'. They call the seven, 'half'. So, you get half of that two and nine for seven hand. And three-quarter of that for eight hand. And when the banana comes here, they hang it up and sell it by the pound. So, when they buy a bunch of banana, they make double the money from that one bunch. So that's how it happens.

When the young Manley became prime minister, he ask them to buy the banana by the pound. They refused. And with them and America they decide to clamp down on Jamaica banana and America went and plant banana in Puerto Rico and Colombia and block Jamaica market. Well, they block Jamaica market with everything. Then they went down to Africa planting chocolate, cocoa. In Ghana they must have at least 100 acres of cocoa. And then they tek the little children dem outta school [to work]. I have been taking notes of all of this!

I deal with the Big Man [God]. Big Man use you! Really, I have an accident, about six years ago. I went over to Sudbury to give out two pair of shoes and then I was going to catch the bus to come back home and this little Indian guy was at the traffic light. He just couldn't wait for the light to change. He drove and then as I was going the wing mirror catch my coat and pull me four yards back way. And I didn't even see de car. I only say, *'What is pulling, what is pulling me, what is pulling me?'* And den when I look, I saw the car then I tried to go 'pon de bonnet. I catch de wipers to see if I could hold dem and to go from the bonnet. And den, de coat loose and sen' me up nearly touch de bridge. And then I drop back on the bonnet and when I drop on the bonnet there was an angel. He's a man. And he catch me. And after he catch me he take this hand and put it around his waist. And when I put my hand around, I think, *'What a man! STRONG!'* And he have a belt on, with studs. He didn't show me his face. I only see from his neck come down to his body, right. And then he puts me down in the road. This is true. Then a black man came on. I gave him my mobile phone. I say to him, 'Take a picture of what's going on for me.' He tek the mobile phone and say, 'Me can't understand it, sir', and him move off and say, 'I wish you well.' And he's gone!

I heard somebody say, 'Call the ambulance!' There was a lorry dat see everything. The man, he stop on the other side. He was going the other direction. And when he saw, he couldn't drive off. He was stunned! I don't know when he was able to drive off, when he saw the ambulance come. But I couldn't get connection with him.

The little chap, he stops afterwards. Then he come back and he take up my head. I say, 'What are you taking up my head for when you want to kill me!' So I put my head down and run. Hehehe! I was laughing and I was all right. And then, when the ambulance came, then it break down. They couldn't do nothing. Then they had to phone for *another* ambulance. And I was nearly an hour, in the street, on my *back* ... before the other ambulance came and they take me up. When the police came, I was in the ambulance. He said, 'What's wrong?' I said, 'A car knock me down.' Anyway, the children dem did get panic and start to ring, so I said to one of the ambulance drivers, 'Excuse me. Just talk to one of me daughters on de phone.' When me look, policeman gone. He went and sen' away the other little Indian guy. And when he came back now he came back wit' his paper. 'Could you sign this?' But he was looking for a dead man. A dead black man. This is true!

They wrote me four letters, the police dem from Wembley. That they are investigating, blah, blah, blah. Den he went and *phoned* the little young man's *father* and tell him, 'Your son have a little accident.' I went to the hospital and they took X-ray and they sent me home.

But Norman's injuries resulted in him returning to hospital for two weeks of treatment...

In the second week, the head doctor came around one morning. His name was Mr Mack. There were six of them. And he said to them, 'Now look on that gentleman – he's 92 years of age [laughs]! And car fling him here, there, there, send 'im up in de air – and look at him in de bed! What d'you think about 'im?' [Laughs.] Dem burst out a laugh!

Thank God I'm here today. I'm 98 now.

I came here because I am making a family now, because I have a wife and children. The mission field wasn't able ... so I said, since there is a change, let me go and try. And then I try and put tings together and I got my fare and I make it here. So I was here before I could send for dem. The wife came a year after, and then the children after that. It takes a little time. Did I behave myself in the time I was away from my wife? I'm always behaving myself [laughs]!

The one thing I tried to gain was some knowledge. In those days, when you came here, it was a place for you to learn. I said to many people, you don't have to go to university when you come to learn, because you *come* to university. Now all the park ... I don't know what I should call them. They were private places after they come on Fridays. So you find all the men going to these different parts on Fridays. Oh my God! [Laughs.] Hyde Park ... there was a place there where they had grass. And it's a sight! It's true! It used to be 'Sale Place'. It used to be 50 pence standing and a pound laying down! And then Billy Graham came here in 1956 and they carried Billy Graham to show 'im what happening in Hyde Park. And the Saturday night he had a service in the studio in Wembley, and his message was, 'This city, is a *bloody city*!' And when he preaches there the night, the following Sunday, from even the same Saturday night, the police dem get on their feet and they had to begin to change the system – they also was in the park! They begin to drive the men out. But they still go in and hide and it gwaan, and gwaan, and gwaan till it sieve out.

The first job I did when I came here was on the building – building and demolition. Labouring. Well, you's in a strange land, you need money to feed your family, so you have to hold on to anything you can. So, I spend four years and four months … oh my God! Out there in the cold.

Anyway, after four years, my second one that I try was the railway [to be a porter]. And then I work four weeks before they send me for my test. And when I went for the test after the four weeks, I didn't know you wasn't to dress or look nice when you go, so I put on me nice clothes. When de doctor man saw me he say, 'Oh this man don't suit this kinda job.' He failed me, sen' me out, for my short vision or something or another. So when I went back to Watford, the stationmaster say to me, 'Every time I get a good person to work, that's what they do in Euston, fail dem.' So anyway, he said to me, 'I'm sorry, but you can only work two more weeks and then I have to lay you off.'

So, I work the six weeks and came back, and then my next job was in a glass factory. When I went there in the morning, there were 13 men in front of me looking for a job. So when the personnel office put on about four or five, he came back and he said – and they were all Irishmen – he said, 'I'm sorry but there is no more jobs this morning.'

So all of dem just left. So, I say, you know what happen, I'm gonna stay, I'm not going. Let me wait a little and see what happen. So, while I was there he looks out again and he saw me and he say, 'Go, go away!' [Laughs.] No, it's true. He say, 'Don't go away, wait. I have somebody I dealing wit', I call you when I ready.' A few minutes after he sent out the person he have, he call me, and he say, 'What can I do for you?' I said, 'I would be very thankful … I'm not working and I would be so pleased if you could give me a start.' He says, 'It'd be a pleasure.' I say, 'Thank you.' And he fill out all my papers and he said, 'You want to start now?' I said, 'No, because my card is at the [labour] exchange. So I would like to go and get my card and then I come in tomorrow morning.' He said, 'You can go and get the card and come back and start work.' I said, 'No. I would like to start tomorrow morning.' [Laughs.] So, he said, 'All right – tomorrow morning you come back and wait for me right here.'

So, I get my card and I went so. The night foreman hate black people! He came in and saw me sitting [in reception]. *'Come out!!!'* He ran me out! Oh, he ran me out like I was a *RAT*! I went outside. Anyway, I didn't quarrel. So when the personnel officer came in the morning and he look over he say, 'Come.' And when I went in he called the foreman and he said, 'I took this young man on', and the foreman look 'pon me and said, 'Yes, yes, yes.' And then he call the chargehand to come and takes me in. When I go in there was a few black men inside. When they saw me they said, 'How did YOU get in here? Who tek you on?' Because a black man mek a fight in there two weeks before, so they did kinda clamp down. They were surprised. And then I go in and I started to work. I worked there nine years and six months. One of my best jobs. British Indestructo Glass. Good wages, by the time I'd just bought this place [in Harlesden] – a whole heap of money – in 1957. I came here in '55 and I moved here in '57.

I worked from eight till nine, four days a week. Saturday and Sunday. They sold the factory to Triplex. Lorries and coach and television and washing machines ... we do *all* of them. And then Triplex closed down the whole factory in 1968. I took a month off. I didn't want to work. Then after the month, in September, I went to Frigidaire and started there. And I worked with them 13 years. The wages was not good but I don't like run about, so I stayed there. And that's where they retired me from when I was 60.

I was here one morning and I took the Brent paper up and I saw a little advertisement that they want – a community group – wants somebody for caring. I said, that's an opportunity, so I made an appointment and I go and see 'em. When I went the morning, I saw six women and they sit all around and they interview me. Six women. And I give them a little laugh! So anyway, after the interview, the coordinator said, 'Can you come back for a review in about a week's time?' When I went back she said, 'Oh, this job is yours. She said there's no one else could get this job but you ... and that smile you have too pretty!' Hehehehe!

She said to me, 'Can you get somebody to write for you a reference.' I came to the minister, Terry, and asked him for a reference. And Terry's wife, she was a teacher, she wrote the reference. She don't ask me nothing – she jus' write it! Because she just look at me and she know me. And when she [the supervisor] got it, she said, 'Mr Mitchell. I have never in my life see a reference like this.' She said,

'I am appalled … the reference that came here for you.' She call a policeman and tell him. It's true me a tell you! Dis man is a good man. She say she told the policeman. *She told me.* She never see a reference like that. I don't know if she did show him de reference. I don't know what the reference say. I didn't ask her for a copy. I don't know what she write. But she surprise her, Terry's wife. This is true what I'm telling you! It was such a reference … me mean GOOD reference! I don't know what she write, but it was GOOD!

They took me on in November. Till January I never get any work. The end of January, she called me and she gave me £25. I said, what am I going to do with this £25? I came home and I wrote a letter to an old lady home and I sent £10 out of that money for her. A little young man did write me for a money – I sent £5 for him and £10 for his father – in Jamaica. A week after that, she call me. I couldn't manage the job dem give me. [Laughs.] I was sent here, sent there. And everywhere I go, everybody want me to come back. And I works three years with them, three successful years.

I was working with an old Jew man over Dudden Hill Lane. I does *everything* for him. He had an accident one morning, he came out and went to the garage, open de door and was putting something in his car when the garage door come down and hit him right in the spine. Cripple from dat.

* * *

In those days were not very much churches, you had to meet at different homes or a hall. Sometimes we leave from here to Stockwell… Brethren would come from Battersea, Brixton, Lewisham and then we'd meet in the Salvation Army hall in Vauxhall, and then we'd have a service. Then during the week if we can meet and have a prayer meeting somewhere and that's how we'd operate till the churches dem organise in this country.

Well, they did not tell me *personally*, not to come. But I went to Westminster Abbey in an evening service and dem move me about four or five times. *That bench is Mr So and So's chair. That chair is Mr So and So's...* So they'd move me, move me till they no bother move me again and jus' leave me! Hehehehe! That's the way the system was here.

This minister, he was the minister for the congregational church at Church Road [in Harlesden]. The church it did get scanty, so they remove him up to another congregational church. And in 1958, McMillan asked him, after the race riots, to go to Jamaica for three months to find out where all these people are from. So when he came back, he made a broadcast and he said the government has made such a mistake that he don't believe it can be correct, because all the people that came from Jamaica to here come out of a church, and the churches turn dem out here. The churches did turn them out. They tell them not to come back. They glad to see them but they running the people out of de church.

The first church I went to was Gospel Hall up in Forest Hill, southeast London. They accept me and they were glad to see me and they invite me home some of them [white people] so I was there a few weeks during the time I was living in Forest Hill. And then after I left and came here I begins to go to Notting Hill Gate and this minister came from Wales. My three children that born here got blessed at that church, Kensington Temple. And then after he becomes old and retired and went back to Wales. So the church was locked up for nearly ten years or more.

There was a set of men that goes there – I don't know how they did get in the church – but they get in the church. And they clean up the place and Kensington Temple become New Testament Church of God! And *everywhere* you go, convention, everything keep in there! And then a white man came in and tell them he wants the church. And he took over the church and so they had to despatch. So ... from they took it over, they have it until now. But the good ting, they didn't stop anybody from coming.

They had a hall in Coldharbour Lane, Brixton. We went there one night and there were more ministers there than members! [Laughs.] This is true! You never seen so many ministers in your life! [Laughs.] And we had a very lovely service. But when de service finish, they have some conversation. Then the conversation turn into confusion. And the confusion that breaks out – we had ministers from Barbados, ministers from Jamaica, ministers from St Lucia, ministers from, oh God, *everywhere.* The one from Barbados he said, 'You know what happens. I won't be coming back here. And I have to find a place to worship. And he went away and he went up to Dalston and he started a church in Dalston, and that is Church of God in Christ. Then another one he started a church in Vauxhall. Then another brother that was there come back and started a prayer meeting on Manor Park Road. All the different churches are Bible Church of God or Pentecostal Church of God or This One Here Church of God! Everybody starting dem little ting. And that's how the Church spread.

The Church in Britain was good. But the ministers in Britain, they look after themselves. There are a lot of tings which the Church could've done but they didn't, and now they are drifting. When the Church was in the early days, they didn't put in the effort to do the tings that should have been done. In truth, they didn't have the knowledge. Because the Church did get so big.

They've started to buy now these little halls and little churches and develop, but you see the main body of people is the British people. And the [West Indian] churches don't have no British people in dem.

You can't be in a church and have girlfriend and boyfriend – that's rubbish. You must keep away from *dat!* I know one of the members … oh, she used to come to my club. My God! I pray the day when she left. Oh Jesus. She went down to work with some people and some of the tenants run her out. A member of the church! They tell her not to come back. She was living next door here and the two young ladies that own de house, they pray the day when she come out.

If I didn't come here, what I've done in life, I couldn't have done it. So it's worth it. I'm everywhere. In Africa … I've been known way down in Australia. I wrote a book [a pamphlet entitled, *The Secrets and Blessings of Longevity*] … I post them free of cost all over the world to people. We give way to money too much and that's why we can't get blessings.

Well, I did come here for five years, myself. Not to go back rich, but I came for five years. But when I reach here, I say you know what happen – I better change my plan! When I went down to Deptford to sign on, I said I'm not going to put 'five years', I'm going to put 'permanent'. I did. Although I did not decide, I said let me put it for surety. And it's a good ting I did. And I'm still 'ere. I here 63 years.

What happen was, we had no cooperation and that's where we failed. We could have done great, great tings here. No cooperation. Many, many of the organisations and many of the social tings that were organised, we have a way of dealing with it … oh, he want to get rich. And any time you hear that come up, it's finished.

I organise a club here and when I organise the club, all the plan that I have, the club was to run from here to Jamaica. I don't even get it to run here as I want it. Because there's no cooperation. I came back here from Canada on 6 September last year. On the last week of November, I closed the club for Christmas with the intention that we start back up in January. Until now it don't start back. Because I took ill the last week in November, with my feet, and there was no one to run the club – right through the year. The hall is still there, waiting on me …. Cooperation. Same ting.

My wife is gone. What, to the other place? No, no, no … she's living in Reading! She's 80. No, no. She's 90. She just had her 90th birthday. They [Norman's children] called me and asked me [to go to her birthday party], but I said NO. Don't bring her back here neither! It's true. I tell my daughter Friday, right there she sit down, I said listen. If I dead, don't carry her come to me funeral! And if you carry her come there and you bring any of the family, the coffin gonna drop off the stand and I gonna roll out before dem!

I build house, give her father, look after her father and her mother and tek up her four brothers here. They come, live and married and live in this house … I don't see none of them! None of them!

Anyway, I took him [the 'Jew man'] to the hospital and when I goes there, I had to undress him and get him ready for the doctor. The head doctor was such a lovely man. He was from Turkey. Sometime in the morning he said to me, 'Do you know how to take water from a man when they can't pass it?' I said, 'No, doc.' He said, 'OK, come watch me.' And he do and now he say, 'You'll do it.' It's true. And I said, 'My God.' The sister, she love me in the hospital. Whenever I go up there she say, 'What you want fi you breakfast?' [Laughs.] Oh my God! I used to live some BIG life! She call me one day, de sister, she said, 'I know you're doing it, but come let me show you how to do it manual.' And me went up and she tek me in and showed me. When he was sick in hospital I have to tek de wife up there every Wednesday and as I go up on Wednesday morning the sister would say, 'Mr Mitchell. Go down the fizzy, the fizzy room and learn to do physio.' You know what – me forget to ask her for a certificate.

I meet some very high people, through that same man, so I respect him. The whole family! Well, I see them so often in my dreams that I think they must regret something. Because he put me on his will. Hehehe! And me ask him for a rise. And he cut me out of the will! [Laughs.] I think it trouble him *very* much, because he knows the care I gave him. But he did leave his hut. He say, 'I want you to get this hut', his bowler *hat*. I did wear it to Westminster [at the Windrush 70th anniversary service]. Hehehehehe!!!

AUNT ENID

Enid Rodie was born in Guyana in 1933 and came to Britain in 1961.
A distant cousin (something I only discovered shortly before interviewing
her), she knew my mother from the 'Guyanese circuit' and would run
into her from time to time. Neither, however, knew they were related.
Perhaps it's a cultural bias, perhaps it's because she reminds me of my
mother, but I love talking to Aunt Enid. Her intonation, her cadence,
the distinctive twang of her accent and a very Caribbean habit of flitting
from one subject to another in quick succession. The written word doesn't
do her justice. Aunt Enid should have her own radio show.

When I came to England I was very surprised to see how dunce and
stupid they were. They didn't even know anything about geography. You
couldn't tell them anything about where you were from. Guyana? They
don't know! 'Wot part of Africa is that?' they'd say, and then they say,
'How much did you pay to get here?' and I say, 'I didn't come by boat,
I came on a flight, the first flight out of Guyana.' It cost two or three
hundred pounds or something. You had all that money to come here.

Growing up, we had lots of stuff because my dad was working at the airbase, working with Americans. And these Americans know that my father got children. We had most toys and all sorts of food – the big tins of baked beans and pork and beans and this and that... My dad would come with a truck full of stuff, you understand? We had a lot of perks.

The notion of coming to England is after I was married, and my marriage ended. I got married at 18, right. OK, I got married at 18 and it last for seven years, and then by that time the last of my friends were coming to England in the late fifties, and I wanted to leave Guyana. Most of my friends was here, you understand? I wanted to come because it wasn't easy for me and my husband. I married at 18. That wasn't young at the time – that was the normal thing ... for some people. For others, it wasn't.

Remember, I grow up in Guyana where Indians was married at eight, nine and ten, 'cause when you marry, you go and live at your mother-in-law, and then they teach you, right? You not sleeping with your husband! But they teaching you to cook, to do housework and all that stuff, you understand?

Since I was growing up, my father used to drive one big DeSoto in Guyana, and used to use that for weddings – a lovely white car. I always said, when I grow big and get married, that's what I want! Let me tell you something, I think you talk things into your life. I never say when I grow big, 'I want a man or I want a boyfriend', or 'I want anything.' Listen to me: the only thing I say, when I marry, when I see that car, I know when I get married, that's what I want! No, it's true! Yes, I say when I get married that's what I want. Listen, the first thing that I book when my wedding was planned was that car because you can't get it – it's always booked up. And I was married on 7 June, 'cause June is a month for weddings in Guyana. So the first thing that was booked was that car. Since I growing up that is what I wanted, you understand? Good.

After seven years, and we separate, I was on my own. He wouldn't leave you alone and following you, and all these ting. It was a bit too much. And we got a lot of ting with the children, and he saying, 'You bring the children', and when the children come, the children at me. And he want the children to go to him. And when the children go to him, the children's not coming back. And he tellin' you come for the children, and *all* sort of ting...

This is how it goes: husband and wife together, and then the husband decide to come to England to make a better life, and he leave the wife in Guyana with the kids, and then he gonna send for the wife, and then the wife gonna come, right, and then they gonna decide to send for the kids... Now we can't send for *all* these kids, you know? Two might come and then the rest is home, growing. In time, they come.

I was fighting to get them all certain letters [visas, etc.], all sorts of things, and I couldn't get my children. You know what they [British immigration officials] told me? 'A wife place is with her husband, a wife place is with her husband.' And if I want my children ... I say well, to get my children, if I got to send for him, they tell me a wife place is with her husband and if I want, I can go back to Guyana.

Praise God that my children were there and when my children went into the immigration [office] they could see the files high up so [points up], you understand?

Remember, in those days, women have children and they workin' in the hospitals. Remember, you's a ward maiden, you're not a nurse. You're a maiden – they the domestics in the hospital. They is now doing the cleaning in the wards and working in the kitchen preparing the meals and some in the laundry, you understand? It's women who's doing that. The men are the porters taking the sick to the different departments and to the wards and all the ting; the dead to the morgue. The men are the porters and the women is doin' the domestics – cooks, cleaners, laundry and kitchen.

I came on the first flight that ever left Guyana for London, in '61. Yes, yes and the flight that I came on we had a bit of a problem. This woman had this little child and she took off the child's clothes and had the child running up and down the flight with only her panties on and the child got sick and the flight had to be diverted. Yes! So we went to Newfoundland. So when we got into Newfoundland, the ambulance was there waiting so they had to take this child straight to the hospital and we were there for however long till we were able to get back on the flight.

Well, everybody save up to get the boat in the morning. I had a friend that wanted to come too [to Britain], and he was in a lot of problem, and my mum lend him the money for him to come. My mum help a lot of people. She lend people all sort of ting to go to Canada and stuff, you know? I lend him the money to come and then when he come then he send back the money to me, that's how I come.

When I came through, my mum had the money, you know, and then I got back the money. Yes, she saved it by throwing bucks. Jamaicans call it 'pardner' and here we call it 'bucks'. When I draw my bucks, I don't want nobody bother me. When I draw my bucks [laughs] I don't want no company – nobody helpin' me spend me money! That is how people get money to buy house, 'cause if you throw two hand [from a well-financed pool], you got a down payment, you understand? That's how they do it.

When I left Guyana, the last one was four, one was about seven or eight ... it was hard, yes, but you're running because your neighbour with the man, but he still won't leave you alone! So, you know, you're glad to be out of there, too. You know all your friends are here and then they telling you, you could come here, and who come here, and the husband was here before, and then they make back up ... I had a friend, she said to me that when she come up, she make back with her husband because it was better for the kids, you know, and all dat. But most of my friends is coming out of there. Some of them stowaway, too, because a lot of these fellas I know used to do it.

When you come and see the condition here ... you say, 'Five year here is enough for me!' It never dawn on me that I could leave my mother and my family down there and come and stay up here, but you know, time passes. A lot of people get trapped because as my friend was saying to me, when you come and they tell you join this and pay for this and pay that ... you never did because you say, 'Why you doing this for so long? I won't be here to stay.' So you never did, and when you catch yourself, you're here 40 years, you understand?

A lot of women, when they came and you go to the Citizens Advice Bureau, then to the Job Centre and they ask you, 'You want to pay married woman stamp or you want to pay single stamp?' and you say you want to pay married woman stamp – one must be 'bout two shilling and the other one might be five shilling – you say five shilling. I ain't paying that you know? But then how much of the men go away and leave the women and when it's time for the pension, because they didn't pay the right stamp they think that they covered with they husband stamp, you understand?

I was living in Fulham: 68 Munster Road. I had my sister here and I had a friend here – the same guy. *All* my friends was here. I had more friends here than home.

The first Saturday morning, we went out to Shepherds Bush Market and everybody's in a huge queue for the fish. Huge queue up by the butcher's. Huge queue up by the greengrocer's and what have you. And all I hearing is, 'Enid, Enid, Enid!' My friend say to me, 'You have spoken to more people today than I have spoken to since I came to this country!' Yes, I know lots of people, you understand? When you going down the road in Fulham and a black person coming, they looking to see for somebody they know, to see if it's somebody you know.

When I came in the spring, the place was bright. At ten o'clock at night it was bright! I went to the cinema in Putney, and when you come out of the cinema the road busy and it's like the afternoon in Guyana! You know, it's confusing. You go to evening show, you come out, and outside people all over the place and it bright, bright!

I was glad to be here. When I reach out with my sister, everybody's there and they asking you, 'Where's Brook Benton?' Because Brook Benton was the top guy at the time, so they want to know when Brook Benton's new tune is out. So you gaffing [having a laugh] and my sister got the house full of Guyanese. We all come up you know, aaaaay waaaa ah! You got your friend's mum and she cooking curry, she cooking curried chicken, and she say, 'Girl, bring me a mango here,' 'cause here all they got is cooking apple! When you cooking your curry back home you put in green mango, you know, and she say but when it near finish you put in the cooking apple!

Well, back home you could only buy a piece of cabbage 'cause cabbage coming from abroad. You buy a piece of cabbage and you put it in the top of your basket, so everybody could see! But here, now when you come, potatoes and all these things are so cheap I could buy a whole cabbage for a penny!

Rice was expensive, then they start bringing in West Indian food like provision, but when you look at it, it's white people that made money from it – black people wasn't importing. They come and working but they know nothing 'bout importing and do nothing, but the white people capitalise on it, you know. They bring in the yam and the eddoes and ting. The people ask, 'Oh, you ain't got this and you ain't got this', and they say, 'No, we ain't got this and now them want this and that', and they find out what black people eat and they just bring it. You got to buy for what price they put on it. You gotta buy it, but if you want it, it expensive!

A lot of Africans were studying and those Africans in those days is the ones that had the marks on the face. Now, you don't even see them. No, you don't see them. The African women that had babies, they were still studying and working. The African women give out the children to these white people in the country areas, whereas we send the children back home, you know? A black person get a baby out, they send it home for the parents then send it when it grown. But the Africans didn't do that: they go home when they finish studying and get their qualifications and they go home and get married and get children, but they left children here when they pay white people money.

Another thing that people don't know, in those days too, in the sixties and all that ... most of the young black women that died here died from abortion. You come from Trinidad and you come from wherever and you come up here to study but if you get pregnant, these white women putting them in tub and giving them gin and all sort of backstreet abortion and killing them, you understand? Lots of the young black women lose their life from backstreet abortion. Go on the internet and find out how many die from backstreet abortion. I telling you, look into it, you will see how much. And another thing I can't understand is how when black people reach the age for retirement they tell you forget your money, go home, you die, they're left out for enjoy the pension.

The first job I got, I went to the Job Centre in Fulham and they send me for two jobs. They ask me what kinda work I do, I say I'm a housewife, right, and then they give me three cards to go for jobs and I went to Sunbright laundry in Fulham by Wandsworth and I went and I got the job. They say when I go and get the job then the other cards, put them through the letterbox and go back to them, so I went to Sunbright laundry and I start working there, about a week after I came here.

I had friends here that give me a raise [a loan] when I came, you understand? You know, so it wasn't bad and then I got a job, so when I got a job at that time, your first pay they say you can get a sub. If you don't have money, you get a sub and you pay it back a little out of your wages every week. If not, if you have money, you say no thanks, you don't need it now. Where I was working I could walk from here to there. I didn't want to pay no fares so that was it. I work at Lemco, which is London Electrical Print. I was a printer, printing condensers, printing the voltage on condensers. It was a big coal and electric company, printing the condensers for everything – planes, televisions, whatever.

I worked mainly among white people, and I show you, when I went to London Electricals they got a long line. When she [the gaffer] come out to choose, she choose all the white ones. They get a job. Don't matter how old they are, they get a job first, then the blacks, Indians, whoever. She choose the youngest out of the set and then the rest she say, 'Well, try again.' You understand the reason for that? Try again because every week they have to take on people because these white people that she take on … the white people do not keep the job because the job is very dirty. The paint do not come out of your nails, right. You doing something, spill it, messin' up all your clothes … you understand? But it's a dirty job. They don't stick it, young white girls that go there and ting for work. They don't stick it. So yes, they don't stick the job, so the people that working and keeping the factory going is the blacks because you got the children at home, you got your parents back home, you got to send money, some people borrow the money to come, you know, so you gotta work, you gotta send more money, you gotta buy stuff for your children.

I would go in the store selling children clothes and I would say I want that, I want that, I want that, I want that, that, that, that, and choose stuff. They take them down and pack it and then I say, 'Well, OK, I can pay two shilling a week, you understand, because this my Christmas box I packing.' So you pick the stuff and you pay every week and then come Christmas now, you get your stuff, you pack your box, then you go to the post office and you post it.

You got your money [from the Christmas club at work] now to send, for your mother to take out the stuff, and for she buying whatever for the children. But every other week or so you sending couple money. You send a pound and it's $4.80 to the pound and that four dollars could feed somebody in Guyana for a week. I tell you then when the pound was worth four dollars and something, you could buy milk, sugar, biscuits, bread, you can buy four pound of flour, you got bread all week, two ounce of lard, two ounce of butter, and a packet of penny yeast … now you baking.

My flat pay when I was working at Sunbright was £5.60 in my payroll, but when I was working at Lemco my flat pay was £4.00 and was piecework, so you had to work for your wages and the more you work the more you get … it was £4.00 basic and then you could work it up, you know.

You work the same hours – there's no overtime. But you gotta work faster, so like me now, when I get a penny more I have my cup of tea or coffee or whatever and I go to work. When ten o'clock come, I don't want no tea break cause I ain't accustomed to that, you understand? So I would sit down to my machine, and that mean that I working. They gone in the canteen and they want smoke; I don't smoke, but then I was

told, 'Enid, you cannot work during your tea break. We had to fight for
it, we had to fight to get a tea break, so if you don't want to go to the
canteen or whatever you don't work, you sit down to your machine.'

Because in this country they had to fight for a tea break, you
can't work! So you go in the kitchen, the canteen, they smoking, you
buy a roll and a cup of tea and you sit down with your gaff, you
know; lunchtime, you walk with your lunch or what have you, you
go in there and you buy whatever and that was how it is. But you
couldn't work, you understand? When you come back and work,
some people are faster than others. You could pull down that handle
on the machine and you got eight stamps on your ting and you ring
… you gotta be fast. You can't laze around all day. You clocking in at
eight o'clock in the morning, clocking out at five. That's it. You go
home, you got your work to do you know, that's it.

Well, how you gonna get on with them [white colleagues] because
when you come through that door, when you all in there you laughing
and talking and singing… We used to sing whilst we working. We
singing and working and all that, but when you come through that
door and they see you out there, on the road, they don't say anything
to you. Yes, they pass you straight. They pass you straight. You're
talking in there, you're not talking out *there*.

You go in there [the supermarket] sharp and you stand up in the
queue and you waiting to give them your money. They put down
your change – they won't give your change back in your hand. And
you standing there and they gonna ask the person behind you what
they want, and that person would say, 'Well, she's in front of me…'
They'd ask the person behind you what they want because they

white. I walk out of places like that. I say they're serving people and I'm standing there and they say, 'What you want?' and serving them and I say, 'Listen, you think I come in here to shelter from the rain?' I'll walk out because they not serving you or you gotta wait on their time.

Enoch Powell and all them. Cho! I went in the paper shop one day and the woman had a big fat cat and all the papers are lined up like this [gestures]. In those days, *The Sun* didn't come out yet. I used to buy *The Mirror*. I just moved the cat to take out the papers and she say, 'Oh no, oh no, you dirty … putting your black hand on my cat!' Then, she catch a fret – she jumped just like how I jump when the doorbell ring! Oh lord, touch the cat! A joke!

You learn to deal with it, you know? They tell you, 'Go back to the jungle where you come from', and then you tell them, 'What kind of jungle would you like?'

I was in Fulham and then I went down to W11, Notting Hill. Then I went to White City and from White City I came up here. In the eighties I went to America and I went to Canada for a while. Then, as my mum was getting older, I went home to Guyana and then I came back and then I went to my son's place and then after I got this place. I been here 21 years now [in southwest London].

When my kids were small, before they came up here, I used to go home a lot. It took me some years before I went back home and then I used to go home every year. I had my brother in Canada, my sister, we all used to go home. I went home and I stay home for a long time when my dad died. I stay home with my mum for a couple of years but I got fed up with the place, with your neighbour, and they carrying on down there, you know? You prefer to be here. You have your children here, your grandchildren here…

I always answer to Afro-Caribbean. I don't put West Indies 'cause I'm not from the West Indies. I'm Guyanese. I am from South America, so I ain't puttin' nothin' 'bout no West Indies you know. That's how I do it!

I show you another thing: this is why the Indians get ahead more than black people in Guyana, because black people just *do stuff*. But look what the Indians gonna do with their children: they gonna buy one fish, they gonna cook the dhal and the rice, and they cook one fish. Somebody get the head, somebody get one piece, somebody get this and somebody can get that. Now black people … now you got to buy a fish for everybody, 'cause you know you can't give somebody the head and somebody a piece of fish and a little piece of tail cause they gonna say, 'What's this?' You understand? But look what the Indians gonna do: they gonna call the boy and they say, 'Hey, boy. We put up money 'cause we want you to study medicine, to be a doctor and so we save the money, right, so we put up so much money we can only spend so much on food and this so you are able to go to university and stuff…'

Listen to me, they explain everything what they doing when he get the food! And if he get a fish eye he eat it contented, everybody eat contented, because they know this is what we get now because it is for a purpose, you understand? They know if they only get a piece of meat, one day will come when each of them could eat a cow, you understand? But you want a cow now, then a time gonna come where you can't even afford rice, you understand?

Guyanese people come to my home, Bajan people come to my home, and people from the islands, and so you fix your table and your ting and they say, 'Guyanese people proper like show off, yeah!' Yeah, because the way Guyanese would do stuff they don't know anything about that, you understand? This is your place for eating: your table is set, your rice is here, your stew is here, right? This is how we grew up. If your mum cook fish or meat or whatever, and you got a bone, she put a plate or saucer for you to put your bones on, you know what I mean? And these people don't know nothing about all of this, so when you putting knife and fork and spoon for stew and your rice spoon and all this they say, 'Oh, God. Why all of this for man? Guyanese people proper like show off!' Show off? We do the right thing and to them it's showing off! I mean, we are doing stuff and so we got a higher ... better way of doing stuff [laughs], better way of dressing, better way of everything! [Laughs.] They don't like it, 'so Guyanese people like show off', that's what they say.

We cook, we got different menus. Back home it's soup on Sundays, you got soup lunchtime and afternoon, you would get some rice and some bread or whatever Sunday mornings, you got your bread and your pepper pot, you know, you got your salt fish and bacon, you got your normal things that come like our stuff. But Jamaicans cook rice and peas on Sundays, stew down the brown meat and whatever they cook, they cook for Sunday and Monday. Saturday they cook soup; Saturday's their soup day. But all this kind of salad and all this different ting, we call that 'side dish'. Side dish: a bit of this, and this fry up here, all this different side dish ... I think we get it from the white people, you understand? Have a bit of steamed this, and this and that, and that's how we go with all this 'side dish' business.

We have all the same stuff: we got the Indians because you got your curry roti, you got your dhal and stuff, and then we have the pepper pot [from the Amerindians] and we got fish, we got fried fish, we got stew fish, we got brown okra, fry up with shrimps, you know what I mean? They don't know nothing 'bout frying up with shrimps.

They don't watch the pepper pot. This just keeps going, all the time, because the staler it is, the better, for months. We got the Chinese – your chow mein, your fried chicken, a nice salad with like cucumber and tomato and basil…

Guyana is one whole mixed-up pot. In those days, Guyana was very mixed. Indians, Chinese, Portuguese … you know we had lots of Portuguese. They had the shops and stores and, you know, business places. Pawn shops and all those things were Portuguese, right, but then after, when they start with choosing the different political parties, yes, then the Indians start to say 'apanjat' [loosely translated as, 'stand together'] and pitch against each other.

I grew up with Indian neighbours, and we all live like one. I don't know anything about that apanjat stuff. That came later. We all live like neighbours, and runnin' and comin' … and if you're sick, your neighbour is there; and if you cook, you give them something; and if you want anything done, they do it for you. You know what I mean? We all live like one till this apanjat stuff – and that just come in because they're more than us [the Indian population].

I first started cooking when I was five or six: rice, stew, boiling plantain, using plantain … anything. Mum used to bake bread every week. You know, she bake for the home. Most people used to bake because it was cheaper if they've got a large family. When she bake, you got your flour and you baking your bread so your bread is going to the baker shop, right? So, you gonna learn to plait your bread, so you plait your little bread up, and put it on the side [of the baking tray]. In those days you could've begged for flour. You could go in the shop, like if you don't have any flour in the house, and you wanna fry fish – 'cause, you know, Guyanese people fry fish. You could run to the shop and say, 'Me Mummy said please for some flour', and they jus' put some flour in the paper and give it. You run home, but then you gotta beg for some salt fish scraps when they cut up the salt fish into pieces. You not baking it at home on your heater; you're cooking on a coal pot. You no have no oven. No so! You go to the baker shop and you pay, whether a penny, a pound or how much, and you take your bread. You gone with your pan. You got your baking sheets and you cover it up well and you take it to the baker shop and the guy's doing the baking. Now everybody got bread!

Guyanese have their stuff. We all together, you know, because you have a sense of your belonging and we all together and we can laugh and talk and laugh about the same thing, 'cause if you from Barbados you might not understand my joke, you know what I mean?

After Lemco, I never work for anyone again – I work for myself. I work for Lemco a good time. I can't remember how long but after, I start to do cooking. I make stuff and sell at home. I give people board, cook for other people's businesses. Catering, yes, that's a fair description. When I start boarding, people say, 'Enid, can you cook for us?' So I start cook, then someone bring a friend, and you come round here. So when you see your friend, you say, 'I'm gonna go and get something to eat … at Enid's', you understand? So, I start cooking black pudding, pepper pot, sous and that sort of thing and selling my two beers, and I making Irish moss and selling that, and then people want my special pepper sauce with the secret recipe…

I never sell at Carnival. I cook for the Carnival. I used to cook for the Mangrove [the legendary restaurant in All Saints Road, Notting Hill]. Yes, I cook the Mangrove food, right. So when I go the Mangrove and cook, we cooking for the *whole* Carnival! I used to cook food and sell every day at the Mangrove. I had the kitchen at the Mangrove – must've been ten years back. I got them gambling downstairs at Frank's, right, and I in the kitchen. So I go in there from morning and I cook, you understand? Oh yes. And then I used to have another guy, this gambler named Peas. He had a place in the West End, and I used to cook for him. So I go there in the morning, he do the shopping and I go there and cook the food, and he pay me daily. Many people who come from work or wherever and then they go there to gamble and he serve food at night, but I cook the food. He used to work in the post office, but they running gambling in the West End and they selling food; when the men coming down there they coming for food, you understand? I leave them say about four o'clock in the afternoon when I finish and that's it.

Oh, well. Let me tell you something: Trinidad make a roti! But I accustomed to Guyanese roti. In Trinidad they call it 'leaf'. But I accustomed to Guyanese roti, so I know always it's better! Then you got your dhal puri. Oh lord, yes. But that's something that I can't do.

I could do lots of stuff, you understand? I do knitting, I do crochet, I do flower arranging, I make wreaths ... but not dhal puri!

I went to Wandsworth College to do flower arranging and all sorts of stuff. Right now, I making slippers. Look at these [Enid produces a bag of shop quality knitted slippers]. I can do more than one in a day. This is what I do. I never sit down with my two hands not moving, you understand? I got a bag here of stuff with all sorts of business. Let me show you...

BERTHA JOSEPH

A two-time Labour mayor who defected to the Conservatives, Bertha Joseph is a radical figure within Britain's black community. Tenacious and vivacious, she has been an outspoken voice in both local and national politics, and a tireless campaigner for the African-Caribbean community since the early seventies.

I left Dominica when I was 17 and went to France, because my aunt lives there. We had French connection. I wasn't sure if I was going to love France – I loved the parties – but I wasn't feeling France. And I had uncles here, in the UK, and other relatives, and they used to come to Dominica. They used to come to St Croix, where my father had moved to, and I came here on a holiday and I said to my aunt that I need to stay here. I started living with my uncle, who was well established. This was 1973. My other uncle was in Whitechapel. One of the things that attracted me was the community. I was so interested in the community.

The only reason why my father didn't come here, when I was four years old, was because he wouldn't leave my mum. My mum refused to come to England. She said I'm not going to travel all that way on a boat; and her dad said, you are married to my daughter but I'm still her father. My daughter is not going to travel on a boat to go so far. I'm not happy. My aunt had businesses in Guadeloupe, Antigua and Trinidad. And she paid for her two brothers to come. She said, 'Go and see what you can do with your lives in England – everybody is going, you go. And she said to my dad, 'I'll pay for you as well.' My dad said, 'I'm not leaving my wife.' She said, 'You can send for her later.' He said, 'I am not leaving my wife for a day! I have a beautiful wife, there's no way I'm going to leave her and go anywhere.' And so, he refused to go to England. He went to St Croix instead and took his wife with him, and then sent for his children.

My mother was extraordinarily beautiful. She was *so beautiful.* Her mum was Carib, her father was mixed race, because his father was a French Jew and his mother was from Ghana. In fact, in Dominica they called her 'Frenchie' because she had beautiful long hair, which she would put in two plaits and then put it back up. Beautiful black hair. She was stunning.

As a little girl, I was very spoilt – but don't put that on record [laughs]. We went on family holidays everywhere. My father worked very hard. He loved his family. He thought they were the most beautiful in the world. He adored his children. Daddy was into buying stuff and distributing in Dominica – mostly wine. What we had were what we call 'dame jeanne' – which are the big, big bottles that you have wine in. Some of it came legally, some didn't. But Dad was very close to the police [laughs]. And he always got it through, whether it came on the boat or late at night at three in the morning on a little boat from Guadeloupe, it came. Dad loved his wine. So, Dad was not short of a penny or two. We were not suffering [laughs]. Dad would say, 'OK, holiday time. Where are we going to go now?' I don't know why, but Dad always agreed with me – he always wanted to go to where I suggested. If I said Antigua, it would be Antigua, if I said Martinique or Cayenne or any of those places. But our holidays were always restricted to the Caribbean because I loved the Caribbean and I wasn't interested in anywhere else.

So, I went to France. It was nice, but I came to England and so how I managed to get involved in Notting Hill Carnival … I said, 'You've got a carnival here? A proper carnival?' And I got involved in Notting Hill Carnival. I became secretary to Selwyn Baptiste.

One of my dad's cousins lived in Ledbury Road, which is right in the middle [of the Carnival route] and I used to go there, and I met Vijay Ramlal – he was involved in the Carnival. And I went in the Carnival office and I could not believe that these were the people who were organising the Carnival in Notting Hill.

I'll never forget Selwyn. Every time he was on the phone he'd say, 'This is Selwyn Baptiste. Baptist with an "E" at the end.' He was so particular about people not misspelling his name. He said, 'Oh, hello.' I said, 'Hi, you're the chairman of Notting Hill Carnival; I can't believe this. So, this is where it all happens?' This was Acklam Road, number five.

There was no time wasted at all. I became Selwyn's secretary and for God knows how many years, and then there was a split in the Carnival, a disagreement. So, I stuck with the Carnival Development Committee and then became the secretary of the organisation as opposed to the secretary of the chairman. So, I was moving very quickly, and started organising Notting Hill Carnival, going to sponsors, getting funding and the split then became quite acrimonious, because Selwyn Baptiste was saying, 'I am the subject matter here – Carnival is my name', and that sort of thing. I was more interested in a very peaceful solution to running Carnival. The way I saw it, if we're gonna fight each other, whilst we're fighting, somebody else is going to be doing something. We need to keep our eye on the ball. We got funding from other sources. I must say, I have always found the London Borough of Kensington and Chelsea very supportive of Carnival. For some residents in Notting Hill, it is the *last thing* they want on their doorstep. Sometimes you can understand why, in that some people are very indiscreet, right. The councillors rely on votes, from the people who live in Kensington and Chelsea. Do most people who come to Notting Hill Carnival live in Kensington and Chelsea? Some live in Canada, some live in the USA, some live in the West Indies, some live all over the place, and therefore, what do you do?

My first *day* job was with the GLC – the Greater London Council. I just applied for a job in the Women's Unit. I was a bit of a feminist. I was well in there, trust me! But the thing is, I am a Conservative at heart, and I have always been a Conservative at heart. My involvement in the Labour Party came about simply because I was helping young girls. I have a passion for young girls growing up properly and having respect for themselves, and I got involved with a Guyanese woman and her daughter – Enid and Pamela. Pamela suffered from sickle cell disease, which was another thing I got involved in. In fact, when I was mayor, the Sickle Cell Society was one of my charities. The Sickle Cell

Society and the Terrence Higgins Trust. And when I was mayor the second time, it was the Down's Syndrome Association.

It was also the Conservatives who had this amnesty for West Indians who came during the Windrush period, to apply for their British nationality – *free of charge* – and to get their British citizenship and their passport, free of charge. All this thing about the Windrush now, and people blaming the Conservative Party is unfair, because it was Alan Johnson who has admitted that *he* was the one responsible for all this.

Let me tell you something. I went to a private school, OK. My father worked and sent his children to private school. If you gave *any* West Indian the opportunity to send their children to private school, they'd jump at it! My children didn't go to a private school because I couldn't afford it, but what I could afford was private lessons. I had a private tutor for my children. I found it necessary to do that. I could've made more effort with hindsight to get my children scholarships, because I could've prepared them for that. So that's one of my regrets in life. My sons have done brilliantly; they've got their own businesses. I am extremely proud. I could die now because my children have achieved. Not just yet because I've got beautiful grandchildren.

The thing is, I am a Conservative at heart. My parents were Conservative. I came here … it was a mistake going with Labour, because they were the first ones to approach me and I was excited. But as the years went by I was thinking, *'What the hell am I doing here?'* I was a damn good councillor on Brent Council. I was an *excellent* mayor. And I'm not saying that to boost myself. But I know from the response that I got from people, and even the response I get now. My ancestors would be proud. They would be very, very proud because I helped an awful lot of people. I still have people tell me, 'Thank you.' I don't remember them. I don't remember them!

There's a couple from Wales who lived opposite the cemetery in Roundwood Road and I met them simply because they wanted to be buried in the cemetery across the road and they were being told that it's full, and they insisted it wasn't and they'd like to be buried there, so they phoned me. I went to see them at their house and I said, you will be buried in that cemetery – they're going to have to find a spot. Thank God, they're both buried there now. So, there's some blessings to come; things are going to get better, right?

But you see, the thing about it is, what people didn't know, I went to their home every Sunday after church to wash the woman's feet, because she always complained to me that the chiropodist didn't come. One of the things I'm qualified in – nobody knows – is foot massage; I learned how to give massage. I did it so that if Clive wanted a massage, I could do it! [Laughs.] Would you believe it! So, I used to go there and massage her feet and look after her and leave and go. Nobody knew that.

I remember once she said to me, 'There was a councillor outside knocking on the door, and he said that he was your colleague.' I said, 'Oh, yeah. Everybody says that.' So, I told him, 'That's our Bertha, we don't need any other councillor thank you very much.' And the guy [Gwyn Thomas] said, 'No, I'm Bertha's colleague.' She said, 'You're not here washing my feet, are you?' [Laughs.] She was 80-something at the time.

I was talking about being a good councillor, but I was in the wrong party. I was voting for things that I didn't believe in. I used to go to the toilet to miss votes. But it is the best move I have made in my life, because the Labour Party ... under Tony Blair I think was wonderful. You'll note that I left after Tony Blair left. But Tony Blair was a good Tory [laughs] – because people left the other parties and joined Labour. To me, he was going in the right direction. I would not be in the Labour Party today with Jeremy Corbyn! Listen, the anti-Semitism and the way he's dealing with it – shocking! People don't know that I have a Jewish great-grandfather.

It is the same thing that they are saying about the Europeans now – that they're coming in with cheap labour. The interesting thing is, how the tide has turned! And now, they're not attacking us. They're attacking the Eastern Europeans for coming here and providing cheap labour. We're not the targets any more. It doesn't mean that I'm happy that the target is somebody else, but I'm saying, we know about it. At the end of the day, when you look at a European, you're looking at a white person, but when you look at me, you see a black person. Do you see what I'm saying?

After the GLC, I went into the private sector for a while, an insurance company in the City. Then I managed the business unit for Southwark Council for 15 years. The unit I managed worked with vulnerable people, victims of hate crime, for instance. A lot of the people from the Windrush era, and living in Southwark, were being racially attacked, racially harassed, racially abused and there are a lot of them in southeast London.

Most people who came [during the Windrush years] were manual workers. There are lots of people who came and went to work on the railways. The unions didn't like them, but the Labour Party scooped them up – you know, we'll look after you, through the union.

A lot of the women I know came as nurses. A lot of them came with their husbands, or the husband came and then sent for them. Some of them became teachers, some of them did cleaning in like doctors' offices, because they didn't want people seeing them cleaning other places, so they were very discreet. A lot of them didn't work because their husbands looked after them, so they looked after the children, and so on.

When I came here I had no sisters, no brothers, no parents, but I had my uncle, who passed away in January. I was pretty clued up, and I was a good girl, actually. I had a vision of where I wanted to go, and nothing was going to stop me. I wanted to join the police force here and become a senior police officer. Law and order is something that fascinates me. What I really wanted to be was a solicitor.

I approached the Metropolitan Police Force, I was accepted, and I was ready to go to Hendon [police training centre], so I said to my aunt in Ledbury Road, 'Well, I might come here for lunch every once in a while, because I might be stationed in Notting Hill...'

She said, 'Oh, where?'

I said, 'Notting Hill police station.'

She looked at me and said, 'The day you join the police force, forget my address.'

I said, 'That's a bit harsh.'

She said, 'How many people have you told that you're joining the police force?'

I said, 'You're the first one. I thought you'd be pleased.'

She said, 'You've got to be joking! People will call you a traitor.'

So, I said, 'Anyway, I have to leave now. I need to go to uncle because I haven't told him.'

'Ha ha, good luck!'

So anyway, I phoned my uncle in Oxford. We were very close. My uncle spoiled me. I said, 'Uncle, I have very good news.'

He said, 'What is that my pet?'

I said, 'I'm going to go for my training; I'm starting my training in Hendon.'

He said, 'Hendon. That's, Colindale?'

I said, 'Yes, uncle.'

'Ah, that's nice. Doing what?'

I said, 'The police force.'

'Hold on, hold on, hold on. You're going to join *what*?'

I said, 'The police force, uncle. And I'm going there, and I hope I have your support because Aunty Doris just told me off.'

He said, 'Well, I second her motion. I'm about to put the phone down.'

I said, 'Uncle, if you ever do that to me I won't speak to you again.'

So, he said, 'Don't phone me and tell me anything about the police force. Because when I was fighting in the race riots in Notting Hill in Portobello Road, I didn't fight for my niece to go and join the pigs. How could you do that? How could you betray us like that?'

I said, 'Uncle, betray?'

He said, 'I never thought I'd get a phone call like that from you. I really have to go. I'll speak to you another time. I'm a bit upset.' And he put the phone down.

So, I went home, and I told my uncle. I said, 'Uncle, I told Aunty Doris, I told Uncle Thomas, they're not happy but I'm telling you, I'm joining the police force.'

He said, 'Well, it's going to be a bit difficult. Some people may not like it, but if that's what you want I will support you.'

I said, 'Really?'

He said, 'I mean, it *will* be difficult, but I will support you.'

And then I thought, the black community is going to turn against me; I'm not going to do it. My uncle in Oxford was so *vehemently* against this, he thought I'd betrayed him already. He came down to London. He said, 'Darling, I'm sorry I put the phone down on you, but I was just so upset. You can't join the police force. You cannot do that.'

So, him and his brother had an argument over it. 'You can't come into my house and tell my niece what to do.'

I said, 'Uncle, it's all right. I'm not going to do it. It's causing too many problems.' But then he sat down and told me, 'What we went through, here, the police didn't support us at all. They were as racist as the people that were attacking us. I stood in a truck in Portobello Market, they were delivering meat, and I took legs of lamb to beat the police with. It was that bad.

'Whether you were Dominican, St Lucian, wherever you came from, you were black, therefore we were all joined together fighting against the racists.'

My heart ... it was terrible for me to hear that, and although I felt I was strong enough to have joined the police force, and get to where I really wanted to go, there was a part of me that felt I would let my family down and let the West Indian community down. You know, there was that unity, amongst black people in this country, and they paved the way for us. It came to physical blows. When you think about black people fighting against racist people here, and the police were meant to protect them, but they were not protecting them. Instead, they felt the police were on the side of the racists … I felt I couldn't join them. I couldn't do it [cries].

If you picture all these people, fighting in a riot against racist people, and the police come, and they are on the side of the racist rioters … I have my own regrets about that. I felt I probably should've joined and then made my point.

Although now, I see the police differently, as I think the police have changed. Even during Carnival, I'm one of the police ambassadors, and so I work with them over Carnival as an intermediary.

Being the mayor was one of the best times of my life. Unveiling the Carnival plaque and seeing my name on it was another one. But when I became mayor for the first time on the 50th anniversary of the Windrush, that was when I learned a lot about the Windrush. People told me stories about having a house and people lived with them and wherever you came from, if you were looking for a room, they'd say, 'Come, come, stay with us.' People would recount their stories. My make-up was smudged, because I was crying.

One guy told me about how he'd bought his house through the pardner scheme. You know, they were all saving, sharing the bills… He bought a three-bedroomed house with a little driveway. He bought a nice car and planted an apple tree and everything. He went and said hello to the neighbours, and everybody was nice. So, one day somebody rang his bell and he came out and he didn't see anybody. 'Oh, I'm sure I heard the bell ring,' he said to himself. Went back in. Bell rang. He came back out. So, when he looked he saw his neighbour and the door ajar. 'Did you see anybody ring my bell?' The neighbour said, "'Ere, some of your apples come over my garden…' He said, 'Darling, any apple you see jus' eat it, it's OK. Eat and enjoy yourself.' Then she produces a tissue and something in it. 'I found a mouse in my 'ouse. Never had any mouse till you came 'ere.' He says, 'Missus, make I tell you sumting. When I come from Jamaica and come 'ere, me never carry no mouse wit' me. So, any mouse you find inna you house, a English mouse dat!' [Laughs.] He said he left and went inside. And this is when the racism started. The minute he bought the car and parked in the garage, the woman got very upset and things changed.

I remember the first time I was racially abused. It was around 1974. It's something that will stay with me for the rest of my life. I was walking on Lancaster Road in Ladbroke Grove on my way to my aunt's. There were two white guys there – one was up the ladder, they were decorating or something – this one guy saw me … in those days I had the Afro… So, this guy wolf-whistles me. I didn't answer. I'm a decent woman – you don't whistle at me. So, he said, 'Go on, you black bitch!' So, I looked up at him and said, 'Black bitch? Is that the same person you were whistling at just now? You can't take rejection, can you?' He said, 'Do you want me to come down and give you one?' [Shakes fist.]

I said, 'Go on then, come!' The next thing, he came down the ladder … but what I didn't realise was there was this Rasta guy around the corner and he heard what happened. He came, and he and the guy went into a *fight*. He boxed that guy!

I said, 'Please, please, stop, don't!'

So, the Rasta said, 'What did you do to him?'

I said, 'Nothing. He whistled, I ignored him, and he called me a black bitch.' So the Rasta started hitting the guy again! Then some black guy stopped in a car. I thought, *'Oh God, I'm going to have a heart attack – don't do it!'* His friend, the other white guy, did nothing. He just stood there and did nothing.

I went to my aunt's house and sat down. She said, 'Are you all right?'

I said, 'There was just a big fight', and I explained what had happened.

'You can't be listening to people whistling. You can't respond. Typical you.'

My experience of the community, the black community, is it's a very loving community. I am very, very proud to be black. I think I am probably the only black person who has left the Labour Party and gone to the Conservatives and the black community still embraces me. It is a beautiful thing ... they may not vote for me [laughs] ... some of them do ... but we do look after each other. You know how you test the love of the black community? Let a hurricane hit. When Dominica was hit by Hurricane Erica, it devastated Dominica. I was at the high commission in London until one o'clock in the morning sometimes. People were coming in, people from Jamaica, Guyana, Trinidad ... threw love on Dominica. We had people from all over, even the police in Leytonstone sent barrels of food they collected. But the people themselves came to the High Commission with trucks, with vans, people from all over the Caribbean offering love to Dominica.

People talk about how we [the black community] don't help or support each other. Let me tell you, when you go to somewhere like the high commission, when Dominica is in distress, and you see people bringing bottles of water, crates of water, they're bringing stuff for Dominica. Black people don't support each other? That's not true.

Things have changed dramatically, which is why we must always honour and respect the Windrush generation, because they paved the way. When I became mayor for the first time, in 1998, everywhere I went I gave praise and thanks to the Windrush generation, because they wouldn't have seen that [respect] when they came here first. They paved the way, they suffered. They went through shit. Although I regret that I didn't join the police force, I'm happy that I stayed loyal to my people, because betrayal is something that I abhor. Some of the community may never speak to me again once they hear I was going to go down that path [laughs].

That Notting Hill riot of 1976 is an experience I'll never forget. What I saw will stay with me for the rest of my life. The 1976 Carnival. It was the first year that I was actually going to play *mas*, in a costume, on the road, with Lawrence Noel. They called him 'Stretch' – because he was very tall [laughs]. In the West Indies, if you have buck teeth, they call you 'Beaver'. If they see you eating a mango for two days, your name is 'Mango' [laughs].

I was in the Carnival office in Acklam Road, on the bank holiday Monday, waiting for Lawrence Noel's band to congregate so that I could go and put on my costume. I was in charge of receiving the money for the stalls and allocating people their stalls … they would say, 'I want dat spat', so I'd make sure they got their 'spat'. I knew all the individuals involved. I will never forget that day when I saw the police overturning the tables of the stallholders, people crying, the police hitting people. It was so terrible. The way the police came out. I'm not telling you what somebody told me. I was at 5 Acklam Road and I was looking out and seeing this happening. Coming from my background in Dominica, where Carnival is something that's enjoyed by *everybody*, it was so hostile. When I saw the police were overturning tables, people screaming, the police hitting black women … I started crying. I could not believe what I was seeing. The people weren't actually doing anything – they were just waiting for people to come and buy their stuff. And there were the police hitting them. The police that I talk about was the police *then*. The police now enjoy Carnival and their priority is to make sure that we're safe. But in those days, 1976 … hostile. I ended up in hospital. I became ill. I couldn't stop being sick from what I saw. I stayed in hospital for two days. This thing made me really ill. The doctor was asking me what was happening and I said all I could remember was the police beating people. It really affected me. I'd never seen anything like that in my life. And the poor black women – how much they had to pay for their meat and produce to cook. I've never told my children about it because I never wanted them to hate the police.

When we came here, we didn't call ourselves 'Caribbean people' per se. We said we were 'West Indian' or from the 'West Indies'. The saddest thing is, I would really love to see a West Indian community centre, here. I know we had a West Indian centre in Earl's Court years ago, which is now where the Dominica and St Lucia High Commission is. We've been here long enough that we should've had a West Indian centre. I'm a very proud West Indian woman. I can approach *any* West Indian person, at any time, and feel that I'm speaking to my brother or my sister. I always feel that I would be welcome. The older generation, the Windrush generation, are the most loving people you could find, and the affection that they give to the younger generation, the pride that they feel towards us, is the kind of love that you would expect from your aunt or your uncle. Because only a mother can give you the love that a mother gives you. But you're getting the love of an aunt or an uncle.

When I became mayor ... my God! The pride in the people. My make-up was being smudged all the time because they were so proud. They didn't care whether I was Jamaican, Dominican, St Lucian .... I was black. I was a black woman. And that made them very proud. When I became mayor, the Windrush generation felt as though they had achieved something and all the time I was thanking them for paving the way.

My uncle was 94 when he died. Over my dead body was he going in a home. It wasn't going to happen. We were going to look after my uncle until he died – and that's what we did. When he was in hospital, I was thinking to myself, if you lot think this is some old man, some old black man that you're going to shove in a corner in some ward, you've got something else coming. The other uncle said, 'I was born Dominican, I shall die Dominican!' And so he did – I covered him with the Dominica flag, as I did with my other uncle. The younger generation has to look after the older generation.

Are black families complicated? Both uncles came here, got married, till death do us part. Do you see what I'm saying? Most of the people I know, their marriages have lasted, or their relationships have lasted. I suppose some people don't talk about their private lives. They talk about their career, they talk about their achievements and so on. And I suppose it's probably the same with me. West Indians are very private people. I have a lot of acquaintances, but if you phone me and I'm at home, I'm probably by myself, or my partner is with me or my children are with me. Do you see what I'm saying? I have never introduced my private life to the world. I have always introduced the former mayor, the councillor, the politician, the Conservative, you know, that type of thing. I think that's all they need to know [laughs].

Britain is where I made my name. This is where I found *me*. I'm born in Dominica, made in England. This is where I had my children, this is where my children grew up, and this is where they looked at their mum with admiration. They always say, 'Thank you, you did so well raising us ... you spoilt us, actually. You gave us everything that we wanted.' They've told me how proud they are of me. But I'm not finished yet. All the struggles that the Windrush generation went through, in this country, for people like me to achieve what I've achieved ... I think it was worth it. I hope I made them proud. [Cries.]

POSTSCRIPT

Many years ago, while interviewing my old *bana*, the rapper, lyricist and musician, Maxi Jazz, he told me a story about how he got into DJ'ing courtesy of the West Indian house party scene. Maxi, like myself, is what I would call 'Windrush 2.0' – second generation African-Caribbean, born in Britain pre-1973. As Nicey and Jenny's story illustrates in the opening chapter of this book, many Caribbean infants emigrated to Britain between the late 1940s and early 1970s, growing up, to all intents and purposes, as though they had been born in the UK. For Maxi, myself, and countless others, however, growing up black in Britain meant having a foot in two camps, a betwixt and between situation that led to large numbers of us later feeling culturally discombobulated. Was Windrush 2.0 still West Indian? Were we British; black British; Afro-Saxon; black, brown, coloured, people of colour…? For a community still wrestling with being strangers in a strange land, a significant bridge between African-Caribbean Britain and 'back-a-yard' was music.

'I remember … my dad giving parties in his house where all the men would show up in suits, usually dark, with a little skinny tie,' says Maxi. 'By about 2:00am the tie would be halfway down the chest, the shirt wide open, a big sheen on the forehead … The thing about those nights was that the conversation would start as soon as the first brother arrived and it wouldn't stop until the last one had left. Never did "these two" start talking to each other, or "these three" begin a separate conversation, or "those four" lock in dialogue. The conversation was room-wide, *all night long*.

They used to cuss too much. But from [one] story would come another, and another, and another. The conversation would be completely free-flowing, and I used to sit there, listening intently. It was great for me, because a) I could stay up late, and b) it was my first experience of DJ'ing, because I would be the one putting on the records. This happened from the age of seven, eight, nine, right up until I was 13. It was great. I miss those days. I miss those days so badly.

These parties were an outpouring, because what I came to understand later was that you couldn't go to work and be black. You had to sit your arse down and be quiet! Don't go attracting any attention towards yourself, otherwise you won't have a job any more. OK, when my dad was working, you could leave one job in the morning and be in another in the afternoon. Jobs were plentiful in Britain at that time. However, you didn't want to be causing no trouble. So it was when they all got together that they could be as black as they wanted, and express themselves fully. And that's exactly what they did.

When I felt like I hadn't had enough attention over the course of the evening, I'd put on one of *my* records, something like Roxy Music or the Stones, just to interrupt the flow a little bit. The next thing, I'd hear: "Eh bwoy, ah, wha' 'appen to you, bwoy? Tell 'im put on some decent music nah." I was, like, *perfect*. It didn't matter that they were yelling at me, I was the centre of attention for a little two minutes. Then I'd stick on something I knew they'd love. "Ah! Ya see? That is de music me wan' 'ear. Where were we?" And they'd carry on. I just needed to be part of it, so people knew I was there and I was contributing to the vibe.'

While Maxi went on to develop his nascent DJ'ing skills into a multi-platinum career, overgrown black kids throughout the country will identify with the pivotal role that West Indian house parties once played as a liberating experience, a talking shop, and a link to a culture being assailed on both sides of the Atlantic. Sadly, that era has passed, but music and singing and dancing remain stereotypically associated with black people. Yes, it's what *we* do ... among other things. But what the uninitiated fail to realise is that these artforms are often abstractions, or even extended code. Whether it is carnival's mocking of slave owners, the social commentary of calypso or hip-hop masquerading as party music, or capoeira's martial artistry concealed in dance, the African diaspora has always found ways to mask modes of expression and communication, for obvious reasons. Such poetry is as much a cloak as anything else.

Arguably, we all put on a front, a costume, a shirt and a tie or whatever, just to get through the day. But how many cultures are defined by a collective ability to disguise themselves, by a need to repackage and reinvent time and time again, simply to survive?

'Windrushers' as they are now affectionately known, have trans-mogrified into something akin to a British institution. Windrushers are not Mexican drug dealers or Polish plumbers or Syrian refugees or any of those foreign bogeymen we have come to fear. In the shadow of Brexit, rising Islamophobia, antisemitism, and old European racism, the Windrush generation has come to the fore as the *good immigrants*. As a benign generation of old timers, they are no longer seen as a threat to British industry, morality or family life. Mainstream Britain can now identify Allyson Williams and Jimmy Ellis as being just like grandma or grandpa. Finally, this generation can be acknowledged, appreciated, *tolerated*. And it's only taken 70 years! As they say, the public has a short memory.

The concept of memory – personal, public and institutional – is at the heart of how the Windrush generation is, was and will be seen for years to come. Whatever was lost, binned, burnt or buggered up by successive governments, legions of faceless bureaucrats probably hoped that sooner or later those at the sharp end of the Windrush deportation scandal would simply go away and be forgotten. But they will not be forgotten. From personal experience, I understand that this generation is, quite literally, dying out. The like of my parents, or Norman Mitchell or Aunt Enid will not be seen in Britain again. One day, all we will have of them are memories. But that is no bad thing.

Shortly before I started writing this book, an old photographer friend, Gerald McClean, recorded his 83-year-old mother, Grace, in conversation with him as the subject of an arts project he'd produced. Having sailed to Britain from Jamaica in the 1950s and, in romantic fashion, met her future husband (and Gerald's father) aboard the ship coming over, Gerald finally got to the bottom of how his parents met. Many a Hollywood movie has been produced on lesser conceits. Talking to Gerald about Grace, I learnt that he had recently discovered many revelatory details about his mother, father and extended family. When I inquired why had she never spoken to him before in such detail about her life he replied, 'Well, I never *asked* her about it in such detail.' The Caribbean mask can slip. Old school West Indians *love* to talk. But are we ready to ask the right questions of them? And are we patient enough to listen to what they have to say?

As I have already lamented, in the slew of regrets I have concerning my relationship with my parents, one is that I never actually recorded any of their anecdotes or stories or rants. Maybe somewhere within my own mini hoard of notebooks, hard drives, antique mobile phones, half-written novels, scripts and sundry ephemera is an old VHS tape or a minidisc with a blast from their past. But I doubt it. All I have are notes, a growing family tree, DNA test results (shockingly, I am *only* 60% of African descent) and some old photos. Oh, and I have my memories. But I often reflect on how the sights and sounds of childhood, decades of conversations, arguments, banter and the like have just disappeared. As someone stimulated by words and sounds, more so than images, not being able to hear the voices of my parents any more seems odd, given the decades I spent listening to their highs and lows, adventures and misadventures. In a world in which everyone's every move is recorded daily and published on myriad social media it seems inexcusable not to record the stories of one's elders for posterity. Today, every son or daughter, grandson or granddaughter of the Windrush generation has a smartphone capable of capturing not just memories, but living history. The cost: a little time and a little effort. And you don't have to write a book about it. All you have to do is show up, sit down, press the record button, and listen.

Acknowledgements

I would like to thank the following people for their help, support and encouragement: Kelly Ellis, Madiya Altaf, Liz Marvin, Ian Greensill and everyone at Bonnier for their ceaseless textual and visual input; Sass Brown, Daisy Buckley, Andrea Parkes and Luca Wetherby-Matthews for their editorial skills; David Howells for working photographic miracles; Danielle, Cosmo and Stella for ignoring me when it mattered most; and Ajuan Isaac-George, Gerald McClean and Aletha Shepherd for introducing me to some wonderful people.

To the contributors who made this book what it is, I cannot praise you enough for your time, recollections, insights and patience.

And finally, to every man, woman and child of the Windrush generation: all I can say is thank you for sacrificing so much and asking for so little in return.